"I've relied on Mike's sage business and financial advice through the launch and development of several high-tech businesses. Now with this book, it's like having my own, private financial guru available at the flip of a page. It's chock-full of no-nonsense, cut-to-the-chase, actionable answers to challenging financial questions I routinely encounter in running my company."
— *William Kazman, founder & CEO, Global Telemedix and iTeam*

"Mike Gonnerman is an understated hero to the world of entrepreneurs. This book sums up much that is Mike — a true expert tied into the different communities that make up the business experience from board members to executives, financiers to accountants, employees to investors."
— *Shari Agatstein, co-founder and CEO, Skelmir LLC*

"Mike has a tremendous command of what it takes to create and run a successful business. He has captured this wealth of knowledge in a book that is a must-read for executives in new companies as well as established companies."
— *Tom Marmen, former CEO, RaidCore*

"As an experienced operating CEO, board member and advisor to venture-backed companies, I found that every question in the book is one that people running high-growth companies are likely to face. Mike's answers are reasonable, refreshing and clear...with no BS or management double-speak."
— *Drew Hannah, founder & partner, Drew Partners; formerly CEO of Parker Guitars and SoftBridge*

"I've been reading the Ask Mike columns for years, spanning one of my startups and a follow-on career as a consultant. His advice in these columns has been invaluable to me. Mike has an uncanny ability to ask the right questions and then offer insightful answers. I plan to keep this book close at hand, right next to my cash flow forecast."
— *Paul Baudisch, co-founder, NetMarquee Online Services*

"When Mike Gonnerman joined Powderhouse as consulting CFO, he helped us get financial clarity for the first time. Now a broader business audience will also get the benefit of Mike's wise counsel and expertise. And it's all couched in that distinctive Mike-style that makes astute business judgment sound like plain ol' common sense."

— Tug Yourgrau, co-founder and vice president,
Powderhouse Productions

"When my business ran into trouble, Mike's magnificent financial model and good counsel helped us keep our heads above water, giving us the runway we needed to turn things around. Without Mike's help, I'm certain we would have folded."

— Ian Agranat, founder and CEO, Agranat Systems
and Wildlife Acoustics

"Without Mike's active participation as a member of our board of advisors, I doubt we would have survived, much less grown to a level that we could be acquired by a publicly-held company. Mike asks the right questions at the right time, and insists on the right answers—everything a strategic advisor should do."

— David Gumpert, co-founder, NetMarquee

"Mike was the first external director and financial advisor for my previous and current companies. His advice, guidance, friendship, and financial model contributed significantly to our success."

— Art Mellor, co-founder of Midnight Networks
and Gold Wire Technology; founder, Accelerated Cure Project

"While he was on my board, Mike Gonnerman came up with several of the best ideas I was able to adopt in running my company. And they weren't limited to just financial topics— he contributed significantly to the success of our sales, marketing and business development activities."

— Peter H. Schmidt, co-founder and president, Midnight Networks

"Mike was a key financial architect in organizing and preparing Eprise to become a great company. His advice regarding finance and administration, coupled with strong cash management and financial modeling talents, were an invaluable resource during the bootstrapping of the company. His help provided the foundation for three rounds of venture capital funding and ultimately a successful IPO."

— *Jon Radoff, co-founder and Chief Technical Officer, Eprise*

"Mike joined the board of LSEnterprises at an early stage in the company's history. His financial models and financial planning were critical in helping LSE get control of its cash flows, establish a line of credit, and set the company on a path of sustained profitability. At the time of LSE's acquisition, Mike played a key role in determining LSE's valuation and provided invaluable advice during the negotiation of terms."

— *Leora Schiff, co-founder and president, LSEnterprises*

"In times like these a clear, unassailable picture of a company's financial status can be the difference between winning and losing. ProductFactory grew up during the most difficult times our industry has seen in the last 20 years and we couldn't have succeeded without Mike's help. Mike brings clarity and unflinching integrity to the table when it matters most."

— *Edward Fields, founder and CEO, ProductFactory*

ask mike

answers to common
[and uncommon]
questions
about
entrepreneurial   michael
finance   gonnerman

Michael Gonnerman Inc.
65 Washington Drive
Sudbury, MA 01776
978/443-1340
www.gonnerman.com

For Betsy
...tqmg

-

Printed in the United States of America. ISBN 978-1-84728-936-0

Copies of this book may be purchased in bulk for educational, business,
or promotional purposes. For information, contact Michael
Gonnerman, 65 Washington Drive, Sudbury, Mass. 01776; 978/443-
1340. E-mail: michael@gonnerman.com.

Preface

When I was still in grad school back in the 1960s, I fell in love with financial models. It was exciting to take rows and columns of accounting data and build a little crystal ball that could forecast the future. Crank in the right numbers and you could see next year's likely revenues, the trendline for market share, the ideal commission to pay the sales force. Very cool, in a geeky sort of way.

I was especially fascinated when the models revealed relationships that seemed counter-intuitive. One of my favorite models analyzed the price of vodka—this was grad school, after all, and we were all curious about this newly-imported drink—and demonstrated that unit sales should actually *increase* as the price went up. Huh? My accounting professor was skeptical, but this phenomenon is now widely understood by most marketers who sell premium goods and services.

Financial models lured me into becoming an accountant (my first job was at Arthur Andersen, at the time one of the prestigious Big Eight), but after 17 years in the corporate world I discovered something even more exciting: working with entrepreneurs. I hung out my shingle as an independent financial and business advisor, and that's been my life for the past two decades.

During this time, I've helped upwards of a hundred clients, mostly technology startups. Yes, a few clients were true bone-heads; they felt number-crunching was a waste of their time and were offended when a balance sheet suggested that their companies were headed for a train wreck.

But the great majority of entrepreneurs I've met have been incredible human beings—fearless, bright, hard working, ethical, and determined to succeed. I've discovered that most entrepreneurs aren't deeply concerned with making money for themselves. Rather, they want to prove that their *ideas* for products and companies are brilliant and likely to change the world. Even when these ideas aren't exactly on target, entrepreneurs create a challenging and ever-changing environment. They force the people around them to re-think basic assumptions and to look at the world in fresh ways.

Perhaps best of all, entrepreneurs never stop asking questions, never seem to worry that they'll "look dumb." Sometimes the questions they ask are narrowly focused on accounting and finance concerns — how to interpret financial terms, how to meet payroll, how much should they pay a vice-president, what reports will their banker expect to see?

But the people who start companies also deal with a much broader range of hands-on management concerns, and I've often found myself helping untangle knotty problems that have little to do with traditional accounting practices. How do we deal with a difficult partner or investor? Which employees are most valuable if we have to cut back headcount? What's the best way to hang on to customers, negotiate a merger, or keep the sales reps motivated?

In fact, running a young company is all about questions like these — and hundreds more. Over the years, my clients (and many people who aren't clients) have asked questions that seem to be overlooked in accounting and business management textbooks, and I've tried to come up with sensible answers. A few years ago, I began sharing some of these questions and answers in a newsletter called *Ask Mike*. Since no one told me to stop, I've now taken the next step and turned the newsletter columns into a book.

I hope you enjoy reading through the pages that follow, and find answers to some of the questions that you've faced in your own business travels.

And if a question occurs to you that I haven't answered — well, drop me a note and I'll see what I can suggest.

Contents

Boardroom Behavior

"If there's no more old business and no more new business, let's declare bankruptcy."

Do I really need a board of directors?

"My wife and I own 100% of our company, and we're in good shape financially. A friend suggested that we ought to have a board of directors, especially if we plan to sell the business in a few years. It seems to me that a board — which wouldn't have any real authority — would just complicate our life. But if we do set up a board, what kinds of people should we bring on board?"

Mike: In a closely-held company like yours, the board's most important role is to give you objective advice about tough issues. For example, a good board can give you a reality test on your financial and marketing plans. They can give you input on major hiring decisions. And when you get closer to a sale, having a few board members who've gone through the M&A process can be enormously valuable.

With that kind of role in mind, look for board members who have meaningful expertise in your industry segment or in key business areas. You want advisors who feel a sense of loyalty to you and the business, of course, but I'd avoid recruiting personal friends — sometimes they turn board discussions into an "us vs. them" debate. If you're really stuck for candidates, try asking your banker or lawyer for suggestions. They usually know who's likely to make the most valuable contribution.

Should angel investors collect board fees?

"We have several angel investors on our board, and one of them has been lobbying to get the same annual retainer that we pay to outside board members who haven't invested in the company. Admittedly, our angel investors are pretty active in helping the company, but isn't that part of being an early-stage investor?"

Mike: I think you've made a mistake to offer a cash retainer to any of your board members. Cash is almost always a scarce commodity in early-stage companies — that's why you brought in angel investors in the first place. You should be compensating non-investing directors with small amounts of equity, and if that's unacceptable you should look for directors who have more faith in what you're doing.

At this point, however, you're probably stuck with your policy of paying retainers. I don't think you have much choice: To be fair, you should treat all of your directors equally and pay everyone the same fee per meeting.

Can the board ignore committee recommendations?

"I'm on both the audit committee and the compensation committees of a venture-backed company. My committees have recently made some fairly conservative recommendations (correctly, I believe), which the board as a whole simply ignored. Supposedly, the board is 'acting in the interests of shareholders' to make the company look more attractive, but I think we're bribing the CEO and booking questionable revenues. Can the board just ignore committee recommendations like this?"

Mike: Surprisingly, the rules are very different for your two committees. Comp committees essentially play an advisory role — they can suggest pay levels (usually based on independent salary studies) but the board as a whole has the final say. If the board feels like giving away the store, there's not much you can do about it.

However, under the new Sarbanes-Oxley Act, audit committees have gained real independence and authority, even in private companies. You're entitled to hire outside experts, conduct investigations, and make recommendations that the board can't just ignore. Audit committee members now have to be "technically competent" to make these recommendations, of course, but if you can document problems with revenue recognition, your fellow board members now have a legal obligation to pay attention.

How do I know if my company is playing fair?

"I was an original angel investor in a startup that took in venture money two years ago and is really starting to grow. However, I'm uneasy about some of our recent sales tactics. (We're paying "processing fees" that look like kickbacks to me). The investors who control the board have basically told me to shut up, and our attorneys have said what we're doing is legal. Is there a way to find out if something sleazy is going on?"

Mike: You're right to be concerned, of course, but it's also possible that these "processing fees" are a routine practice in your industry — and are considered ethical by everyone involved. Every industry has gray areas like this, and you should probably start by talking to a few industry veterans about your concerns. You'll find out very quickly if there is an ethical issue that's worth a confrontation.

As a board member, you should also be getting advice from your auditors about how other firms in your industry handle such matters. That's one reason it's always a good idea to hire financial advisors with specific industry experience: There's a good deal of "common law" in most industries that defines legitimate business behavior, but you won't find these rules in accounting textbooks.

Am I just a rubber stamp?

"I'm on the audit committee of three fairly young companies, and I'm a bit spooked by the Enron situation. I'm pretty sure the numbers I see are legitimate — all three companies are run by people I trust — but in the end I'm just rubber stamping reports that management has given me. Is there any way, without a lot of trouble and expense, to get some independent verification of our financials?"

Mike: You're right to be concerned, but your top resposibility as a director isn't to verify the numbers (that's what auditors do) — it's to make sure the company has the right internal controls and the right people to keep the numbers trustworthy. You might want to set up an unofficial meeting with the auditors and ask for their assessment of the company's financial reporting. If there are any hidden issues, they'll find a way to warn you.

Another way to check your numbers is to compare the company's financial statements against standard industry ratios. For example, an unusually high receivables ratio is often a red flag that the sales force is booking semi-fictitious deals; low inventory turns might suggest that the balance sheet is padded with a lot of unsalable (or non-existent) products. Even if the numbers turn out to be real, you'll help keep management honest by asking why their peers seem to get much better results.

How do I tell when accounting is "conservative"?

"Over the past few years, I've been a board member of three companies and invested in a dozen more, all of which claim that their accounting is 'conservative.' Is there a simple test — a balance sheet ratio, say, or a revenue recognition method — that indicates conservative vs. aggressive accounting? Or is this just hot air?"

Mike: Sadly, there's no easy test of "conservative" accounting — which is perhaps why boards are occasionally shocked to hear bad news from their auditors. The next time a financial executive from one of your companies claims to be especially conservative, try asking what he actually means. Chances are, you'll get a long-winded and evasive answer.

If you really feel like digging into this question, however, one good test is to look at the quality of the assets on a company's balance sheet. If the company treats hard-to-sell inventory and long-overdue receivables as full-value assets, that's hardly "conservative" accounting. The same is true of balance sheet liabilities: If you find understated reserves for returns, debt to investors that's treated as equity, or deferred revenue that's been booked prematurely, that's usually a sign that management is being way too aggressive in their accounting practices.

How should our board set the CEO's pay?

"I was recently appointed to the compensation committee of a pretty successful startup (so far, at least). I feel we should give the founder/ CEO a hefty raise, because he's doing a great job. But the other board member on the committee says the CEO is 'just a hired hand' who doesn't have any of his own money at risk, and therefore doesn't deserve exceptional pay. We're deadlocked. Your opinion?

Mike: In a sense, your CEO is playing a double role: As a manager, he's a hired hand who should be paid a market-rate salary for doing his day-to-day job. But he's also an entrepreneur whose efforts can help drive the return realized by the investors. My advice is to develop a compensation plan that's heavily weighted toward incentive pay — that is, the CEO should get exceptional pay only if there are exceptional returns for the investors. This usually means a plan that's heavy on the equity side (options, restricted stock, etc.) and light on cash.

Of course, you should be aware that founders don't always feel this way. Often, they've struggled for years to get their companies properly financed, and then they see brand-new hires getting paid highly competitive salaries by the investors. Telling the founder to make further sacrifices can be demoralizing, so make sure the incentives you offer are really attractive and not impossible to achieve.

What's a fair cash payment for an advisory board?

"I'm trying to set up a board of advisors for my company, but I don't want to give out stock for their participation. Is there a rule of thumb for how much I should pay?"

Mike: Most companies prefer to pay their outside advisors and board members with stock, but if it's unlikely that the stock will ever become liquid, it makes sense to pay cash. Typically, advisors are paid about $5-$10,000 a year for their services—more, if you ask them to perform tasks (research, detailed analysis, recruiting) that you'd usually pay your own employees or outside contractors to handle.

One question you should address is *when* this fee is paid. Stock generally vests once a year, so you may want to pay your advisors annually, like a bonus. However, if you hold regular advisory board meetings—for instance, once a quarter—it's a nice gesture to hand out checks at the end of the meeting, along with a personal thank-you for their contribution.

Your Friendly (?) Banker

"Sure we have mortgage money. It's just that you can't have any."

What will make my bank happy?

"My bank just turned me down for what I thought was a very modest credit line (we'd never borrowed a dime before). We've been operating for a long time, more or less in the black, so I'm confused. What is the bank really looking for?"

Mike: It isn't usually the size of the loan that matters to a bank — it's the risk factor that they care the most about. These days, banks are looking for an almost guaranteed way to earn interest income. When you say you've operated "more or less in the black," that's a red flag to a bank that you may on occasion have problems repaying the loan and the interest. The bank will protect itself with personal guarantees, collateral (which can mean substantially all the company's assets, including intellectual property), and covenants (financial ratios) that you must meet. But these are just a safety net. If the bank isn't comfortable with your ability to repay the loan — and, more subjectively, with the character of the key people on your management team—they'll almost certainly decide the loan is too risky.

What happens when a partner goes bankrupt?

"One of my three partners is on the verge of personal bankruptcy. The four of us have personally guaranteed a hefty company credit line, and we're concerned that we'll get dragged into a messy situation. Our lawyer says we should just dissolve the partnership, but our banker insists we'll still be jointly responsible. Help!"

Mike: At the risk of preaching, this is exactly why personal guarantees are dangerous, especially when they involve joint liability. If one, two, or more of the guarantors on a loan can't pay, banks will go after whoever has the deepest pockets. That's their right.

But your situation may not be as dire as it seems. I assume the partnership has kept the loan current, so the bank almost certainly has no reason to insist on immediate payment (though you may be encouraged to pay it off more rapidly than you planned). Sit down with your loan officer as soon as possible and see what you can work out. Remember—the bank doesn't want you to default, either.

Why can't we find a banker who'll stick around?

"My CFO and I have read all the books and articles about the importance of building good banking relationships. But our bank is a revolving door — the officers never stay for more than a few months, and during that time all they care about is pitching inappropriate services and talking us into refinancing whatever deal we signed with their predecessor. Are we doing something wrong?"

Mike: No, churn in the banking industry is a significant problem these days for many companies. To start, you might want to raise this issue with the head of your local bank. Tell him you're dissatisfied with the turnover on your account and you expect him to assign a lending officer who'll invest time in getting to know you. Be clear that you'll move to another bank if the bank manager doesn't follow through.

Incidentally, the books are absolutely right about the value of a good banking relationship. I remember working with a company that had lost a major account and couldn't meet its next payroll. The company wasn't in compliance with its bank's lending covenants, and everyone was feeling desperate. Their banker stepped in, increased their credit line, and helped them work out a plan to raise cash by selling part of the business. That's the kind of banker you want in your corner.

Why does my personal credit matter?

"Our bank wants me to personally guarantee our new corporate credit line, which I've agreed to do – very, very reluctantly. However, now the bank is saying that my own credit is an issue, probably because I take a minimum salary and have most of my money tied up in the company. Are they just jerking me around?"

Mike: No, it's pretty standard practice for banks to base loans to smaller companies on personal credit, even though the loan is supposed to be based on business assets. In fact, many banks will check the guarantor's own credit score (as compiled by Equifax, Experion, or TransUnion, the three major credit rating services) before they pay much attention to company financials. That's especially true if the business is new or thinly capitalized.

There's not much you can do if you get a failing score, unless there's information in your file that's simply wrong. But you can at least get a preview of what the bank sees by going to the Web (http://qspace.iplace.com), where you can retrieve your personal credit history and score from the three large credit agencies. Once you see how you stack up, you'll be in a better position to evaluate the bank's position and perhaps to convince them that you're a better risk than they think.

How can we clear checks faster?

"We have an out-of-state client who sends us monthly checks for $20,000 each. Trouble is, the checks take at least two weeks to clear.

The client says the money leaves his account the day after we deposit the check, so what's going on here?"

Mike: Banks have a legal right to put a hold on funds in case a large check bounces, but some banks — probably including your own — are clearly abusing this right. One solution might be for you to open an account at your customer's bank (which might have a branch near you), which cuts your own bank out of the loop. If necessary, you can even express mail the checks back to the branch that issued the check and then wire the funds back to yourself the next day. It's a hassle, but you can probably get the turnaround time down to just a few days.

You might also try talking to your customer about the problem. They might be willing to send you a certified check or wire the funds directly to your bank. If you're an important vendor, they should be happy to do you a small favor like this.

Living With Partners and Investors

"You're a partner now, Cosgrove. Partners don't do self-deprecation."

How can we get rid of an inactive partner?

"I have a partner who no longer plays any active role in the business and doesn't collect a paycheck. However, he does use a company credit card very freely for personal expenses. He says he doesn't want the rest of us to buy him out – this is just a 'dividend' for his equity. Is there any way we can resolve this situation without a legal battle?"

Mike: It doesn't sound like this marriage can be saved and you don't have the partnership equivalent of a prenuptial agreement, so it's up to you to take the initiative. I suggest you immediately cancel his company credit card, inform him that you'll be issuing a 1099 information return at year end reporting his non-business charges as income, and begin negotiations (better to call them "discussions") to buy him out. It's possible the negotiations will get ugly, but there's zero chance your partner will make a graceful exit if he's still collecting cash from the company.

Can I object to corporate donations?

"About a year ago, I sold two-thirds of my company to a couple of investors. We get along well, and they've really helped turn around the business. But now they've announced that their religion requires them to donate 10% of our total corporate profits to their church. I suppose they have the power to do this, but I'm not happy about handing over a chunk of my profits to a church I don't even belong to. Can a minority shareholder object to corporate donations that obviously have no business purpose?"

Mike: There's no easy answer to this question, in large part because so many companies routinely make donations to "good causes" and even political parties without consulting their shareholders. Since these donations don't benefit the company or shareholders except in very indirect ways, you could argue that charitable gifts constitute "egregious" spending the same way that paying for lavish parties by the CEO should be unacceptable. It's not a religious issue — rather, it's a simple matter of fiduciary responsibility.

Usually, donations don't have any material impact on the company's profitability, so shareholders rarely object. In your case, however, a 10% reduction in profits is certainly meaningful. You have three or four possible choices: Accept your partners' tithing as part of your loss of control of the business, take them to court (a bad choice), or offer to sell your share of the business — preferably at a price that reflects the company's recent successes. You might also tell your partners that you're bothered by the tithing decision, and ask them to pay your share of the 10% donation out of their own profits. It's a long shot, but if they refuse you'll at least know if the issue is negotiable.

What happens if we can't agree about priorities?

"We sell software to lawyers, who have almost zero interest in being on the cutting edge of technology. Our two core products are essentially finished — virtually no bugs or features anybody has requested. I think it makes sense now to cut our R&D budget way back and invest the cash in sales, but my partner (a technology

*guru) says we should be investing in new products that could
expand our market beyond the legal niche. Your advice?"*

Mike: Since discussions like this can become very emotional,
you and your partner should try to analyze your two
strategies as if they were simple investment decisions — which
they are. Build a set of financial projections, both near- and
long-term, to compare the likely impact of technology and
sales investments on your revenues, cash, and shareholders'
equity. Use your historical experience — for instance, revenue
per salesperson or the fully-loaded cost of a software
developer — to make your forecasts as objective and accurate
as possible.

In general, you should look for revenue growth in two or
three years of 25-30 times the dollars you invest today in
either technology or sales. If there's no way your forecast gets
you to that kind of payback, you might also want to look for
investment opportunities outside your own company.

How can we attract small investors?

*"My partners and I run a small, profitable software company with
growing revenues. We see some serious growth opportunities, so
we'd like to bring in a few investors in the $100,000 to $1,000,000
range. We have a business plan that many people say is well-
written. But our one shortcoming is that none of us is any good at
schmoozing investors. Would you recommend that we pay an
outside expert a finder's fee to help us?"*

Mike: Absolutely not. Investors aren't dumb — they don't
hand over big chunks of cash because they've been snowed
by a slick business plan or because an "outside expert" set up
a meeting. In the end (and this is something I've seen with
dozens of venture-funded startups), investors get excited
when they see lots of customers knocking at your door. If you
can pass that test with flying colors, schmoozing doesn't
matter.

Of course, you will need a business plan eventually, if only to
put down on paper a basic outline of how the business works.

But especially these days, investors aren't much interested in theoretical numbers or cool products. They want to see evidence of explosive growth, and the only way to provide that evidence is to keep making real sales to more and more real customers.

Should we discuss our cost of capital?

"I hired an MBA to put together a financial presentation for a venture firm we hope will invest in us. He's put in terms like IRR, EBITDA, and WACC. Since I have no idea what these things mean, I feel awkward about making the presentation. What should I do?"

Mike: Don't worry about it. These terms are used by big, mature companies that have very stable financing options. Venture investors will look at how fast your revenues will grow, when you're likely to turn profitable, and how much cash you'll need. If they see a realistic chance to increase their investment significantly (say, ten-fold or more) within two to three years, that's what counts.

By the way, IRR stands for "internal rate of return," EBITDA is "earnings before interest, taxes, depreciation and amortization," and WACC is your "weighted average cost of capital." Just in case anyone asks, now you know.

Should I pay commissions to a VC group?

"A venture capital group has offered to raise $3 million for our company by selling 20% of the business. That's a valuation of $15 million for the whole company, which I think is absurd, but they'll work entirely on commission (15% of whatever they raise), so I can't see any downside. Am I missing something?"

Mike: Very little about this deal passes the sniff test. First of all, true venture capital firms don't charge finders fees for making investments. They expect to make their money from the long-term success of their portfolio companies, and to some degree from fees they charge their own fund participants. Even when a investment group raises money for a company, moreover, a 15% commission is unusual. The so-called Lehman formula is more standard — 5% of the first $1 million, 4% of the second million, and 3% of the third million. That's about a quarter of the fee your group has proposed. And you should expect to write a big check for legal and closing fees as well, and probably for all the out-of-pocket expenses that your "venture capital" group runs up.

Then there's the issue of the "absurd" valuation. With a little smoke and mirrors, a fund-raising group might be able to convince unsophisticated investors to overpay for your stock. But then what? The next time you try to raise money or sell any of your own stock, new investors will almost certainly "ratchet down" the price to something more realistic. Your first-round fund-raisers will have collected their commissions up front in cash, and you'll be left with a very angry group of badly-diluted shareholders.

What's wrong with royalty-based financing?

"An investor has made a very tempting offer — he'll give us the cash we need for a new product, in return for a 10% royalty on every unit we sell for the first eight years. If the product sells well, we'll end up paying a huge amount in royalties. But if it flops, we have no real exposure. Is there something here I'm not seeing?"

Mike: You're right to be skeptical. If you read the royalty agreement carefully, you'll almost certainly find that it calls for a fixed minimum royalty in case the product price is discounted. This sounds like reasonable protection for an investor, but it also means that you'll be paying a much higher royalty percentage — perhaps as much as 50% — whenever you sell the new product at a lower-than-anticipated price. That minimum royalty could prevent you from closing large OEM deals or from dropping your price to grow unit sales more aggressively. A lot can happen over eight years, and you need all the pricing flexibility you can get.

Even if you aren't faced with a minimum royalty (rare, but possible), you'll still be committing 10% of your sales revenue to a cost that can't be reduced no matter how well you run the business. That 10% could easily represent your entire profit margin, and it's a handicap that no competitor will carry.

Do I have to tell investors everything?

"I'm about to bring in some much-needed venture capital, but first the VCs are insisting on a 'forensic' audit — they want the right to look at every contract, every bit of private correspondence, every bank statement from the day we started. We run an honest business, but there are a few deals I'd rather keep secret. What can I do?"

Mike: It's not an unreasonable request. While you may want to keep secrets from your wife, you can't do that to prospective investors. You should discuss any "secret" deals before they begin their due diligence, so you can explain the circumstances. Your investors probably won't care about past history (unless it reveals something negative about your character or judgment), but they certainly deserve to know about deals that might limit the company's growth or margins going forward.

Incidentally, full disclosure should also be the rule even after the due diligence period. Your investors will always expect timely, accurate and full disclosure of how you're running the business. If you try to hide bad news and secret deals, you can expect to change careers once your investors learn about what's going on.

Debt or equity?

"My angel investors have decided that their future contributions will be made as 'loans' at a 10% interest rate. Their explanation for this arrangement sounds like double-talk to me. How can someone invest money in a company and still call it a loan?"

Mike: The short answer is, they can't. Debt and equity often get confused, but the simple accounting test is that if a company has the right to repay the amount advanced, then it's categorized as debt. (By the way, that includes most of the preferred stock investments that venture capitalists make, which typically provide for redemption.)

The fact that your investors are getting stock as part of a loan package isn't a problem, at least not from an accounting perspective. But be very careful how you book their contribution on your balance sheet. I know of at least one large company that had to go through an embarrassing financial restatement because it was treating investor loans as equity. You can imagine the red faces when the founders tried to explain to their bankers why a few million dollars in equity suddenly turned into liabilities.

What if we can't afford first-class legal and audit services?

"My three partners and I have been working without salary for a year and trying to save every penny for growing our business. We're doing pretty well — almost a million dollars in revenues from three solid clients. We're ready to bring in investors, but a couple of people we've approached say we need 'professional' legal and audit services. That's an expense that's hard for us to justify: We'd rather put the money into something more productive, or even pay ourselves. Can't we wait until after we raise more money?"

Mike: I suspect that your prospective investors are concerned with the quality of your legal and accounting services, not just the name and reputation of your advisors. You don't want to make mistakes when you set up a company's corporate and financial structure, because these mistakes always come back to haunt you (and your investors).

Bear in mind that there's a good deal of competition for new clients, even among top-tier lawyers and accountants. I suggest you discuss your needs with several firms and tell them you'd like to be billed at sharply discounted rates in exchange for a long-term relationship. That's a reasonable request that almost everyone will consider.

One other point: Until you can afford to pay yourselves and your service providers at market rates, you really don't have a viable business — and that fact will be reflected in your discussions with investors. You might be better off waiting until you've built up your revenue base and made a profit before you take outside capital.

How do I measure dilution?

"I need to talk to my investors about an additional financing round, but first I want to be clear about how to measure dilution. Should I take into account shares that were authorized but not issued? And what about option grants that haven't vested yet? Or is this something we're just going to haggle over?"

Mike: The formula is complicated, and someone always seems to get caught by surprise during a financing round — including experienced investors. The basic rule is that the fully-diluted shares outstanding before a financing include (1) all the common shares issued and outstanding, (2) all the common shares committed (options and warrants, including those that have not vested), and (3) the common shares that are issuable upon conversion of any preferred stock that's outstanding.

Check carefully to see if any of your preferred stock agreements provide for full or partial anti-dilution protection. If so — and this is a common situation these days — you could have to issue more shares to your current preferred shareholders if the next preferred financing is a "down round." Anti-dilution calculations are very complex, and I've posted a special calculation tool on my Web site (www.gonnerman.com) to help you run the numbers.

How do investors feel about high-living managers?

"Our executive team has set up a very generous benefits plan for itself — luxury car leases, open-ended expense accounts, fancy office furniture, etc. I'm trying to put together a business plan to attract some expansion capital, and I'm worried what investors will think about our high standard of living. 'It's a sign of success,' my boss says, but I'm skeptical. Your opinion?"

Mike: You're absolutely right to challenge extravagant spending. There may be some advertising value to looking successful — for instance, if clients regularly visit your offices — but most of us can easily spot out-of-control spending when we see it. Is there any business benefit to holding a board meeting in Bermuda? For paying first-class airfare for all executive travel? For holding a Christmas party at a ritzy restaurant? Probably not.

Investors are particularly hostile to lavish spending, because they feel management has a single objective — to create value for the owners of the business. They'll accept a modest level of creature comforts, especially if it helps attract talented executives. But you can expect to be challenged on any major expense that doesn't have a clear connection to shareholder value.

The Founder's Perspective

"Let's face it: you and this organization have never been a good fit."

What's my equity worth?

*"I own 25% of a service company with a few big, stable clients —
very profitable, but not much growth potential. I've decided to sell
my equity to my three partners, but we're stuck on how to figure a
price. My partners don't want an outside buyer, so there's no
'market' to use as a yardstick. Can you suggest a formula?"*

Mike: The rule of thumb for service companies is that
they're worth 80%-200% of the trailing 12 months revenues. A
potential outside buyer might argue for 80%, citing your
reliance on a small number of customers; the seller would
shoot for the 150-200% range, arguing that your high profits
and low client turnover deserve a premium. Starting with this
range, you and your partners should try adding up the
plusses and minuses of the deal to see if you can agree where
the most reasonable multiple falls.

To test this decision, by the way, you might try calculating the net present value of the cash distributions (salary, commissions, draws and dividends) you'd expect during the next five years.Then subtract the likely cost of your replacement, if the business can't operate without your services. The net amount should be somewhere between the 80% and 200% of revenues, and can serve as a reference point for your discussions.

Do investors want me to put my own money at risk?

"I've been talking to potential investors, and I'm getting very mixed messages about how much cash they expect me to contribute. One investor says I should have 'skin in the game' (his term) to make sure I protect the company's assets. Another says he doesn't want me to worry about personal losses if we decide on a high-risk strategy. Which is more typical?"

Mike: It's not unusual for investors to ask founders to take part in financing small, early stage deals, especially when total cash into the company is less than $750,000 or so. For larger deals, founders are rarely able to kick in more than a token share of the company's total capital needs — and professional investors often feel that it's a nuisance to have small shareholders involved in financing decisions.

Even if your investors do want your participation, you should be very cautious unless you're a sophisticated investor and understand the fine points of preferred stock agreements. You're already making a full-time commitment of your time and entrepreneurial skills to leverage the contribution your investors are making. It's unrealistic to ask you to risk your own money as well.

How much founders stock do I deserve?

"I've been helping a friend get a software startup off the ground. He and a group of offshore programmers have written all the code, and I've provided some necessary expert content. I've also lined up our first major customer and found a group of investors. Now we need to figure out how my contributions translate into a percentage of the company. Can you suggest any guidelines?"

Mike: As a starting point, you might look at the amount of equity a funded startup would give employees who were hired for each of these functions, then adjust the total to reflect the higher risks of working for an unfunded startup. Typically, a venture-funded company will pay around 0.5% for a significant technical hire, 2%-5% for a vice president of sales and marketing, and 0.5%-2% for a CFO—essentially the roles you've filled so far. Thus, your contributions would be worth anywhere from 3% to 7% in a funded company, or probably about 5% in total.

You can legitimately triple or even quadruple this amount to adjust for pre-funding risks, which would translate into a 15%-20% share of founder's equity. Of course, that's only a very rough calculation. Your share should also reflect any salary you're going to get, any other contributions you've made as a co-founder (moral support is sometimes worth a lot), the number of other equity partners, and other factors. You and the other co-founders should also expect that your equity will vest over time, usually four years, to make sure you continue to make significant contributions to the business.

Can I license my intangible assets to a new company?

"I'm hoping to raise money for a new company that will use technology and customer lists that were originally developed for my current software business. Trouble is, investors have been unwilling to assume any of the software company's liabilities (mostly a bank credit line and trade payables). Would it work if the old company licensed its assets to the new company, in return for royalties that could be applied to the liabilities?"

Mike: Your creditors—in particular, your bank—almost certainly consider your company's intellectual property assets as collateral for the company's liabilities. If they go along with your licensing plan, it's likely that your creditors will insist on some pretty stiff personal guarantees from either you or your investors. And even then, the new company could end up losing access to your IP assets if your current company defaults on paying the bank. Royalties always look like an easy financing mechanism—until you miss your revenue forecasts and the royalty stream dries up.

Was I diluted or deluded?

"I joined a small startup team as chief technology officer (mostly unpaid) in return for 15% of the company. Now, after six months, the company has brought in investors and new employees, who are all getting lots of new shares. I'm now left with less than 5% of the company. Shouldn't the founders give me the percentage I was promised?"

Mike: Equity shares are always a moving target. When you first joined the company, you should have received a formal, written document that spelled out your share of ownership at that point in time. Many co-founders feel they can get started with just a handshake agreement, and sooner or later they run into exactly the problem you now face.

Accountants & Other Odd Characters

"The whole fun of accounting was that willingness to suspend disbelief."

How much time should it take to close my books?

"I'm having a running argument with my controller: It takes him at least three weeks to put together financials for the previous month, and that's just not fast enough. A few times we've had ugly problems that we found only after it was too late to fix them. Is everyone else flying blind, too?"

Mike: You're definitely not alone, and the problem is getting worse for everyone who tries to operate in a "just-in-time" mode of lean margins and less cash in the bank. Fortunately, this is a pretty easy problem to fix.

Most important, you need to make sure your controller is processing transactions much faster. In fact, daily posting is best, especially for big-ticket items like customer payments and vendor invoices. You'll probably find a lot of your own in-house transactions—like bills to customers and payroll—also aren't getting in the system as quickly as they could. (For instance, if you use a payroll service, you'll typically get a detailed statement a day or two before the checks are cut.)

Of course, there will always be a few vendor bills and other odds and ends that drift in late. Your controller should be able to post pretty accurate estimates from purchase orders and past history; if his estimates are consistently off, that's a problem all by itself.

Once you're posting transactions on a daily basis, you can ask your controller to prepare daily or weekly flash reports that show key operating information. And you can also have him run month-end reports on the very first day of the following month. He'll have to make later adjustments to actually close the books, but this process will certainly uncover major problems almost instantly.

What's better — a CPA or an MBA?

"My partner and I have decided we need a CFO for our company, which now has $3 million in sales and is growing at 25% a year. My partner wants someone with an accounting background; I'd like an MBA type. Who's right?"

Mike: This is a tough call, because the ideal CFO candidate should be strong in both areas of expertise — technical accounting and general business savvy. However, financial executives with a joint MBA/CPA background are relatively hard to find and command much higher salaries than a $3 million company can probably afford.

If you have to choose, my advice would be to look for a candidate who's strongest at accounting, since the most important contribution a CFO can make is to "get the numbers right."

Are my controller's mistakes normal?

"I happened to look through a printout of last year's general ledger, and it's full of transfers from one account to another, refunds from double payments, and other evidence of careless mistakes. My

controller insists that mistakes like these are normal and don't affect our final numbers. Your opinion?"

Mike: Everyone makes mistakes when they write checks, but it's easy to tear up a personal check for the wrong amount. Accounting systems are less forgiving: They keep a permanent record of every adjustment and transfer. Although this is an important security feature, mistakes really stand out. You need to decide how often your controller is really making mistakes. If he's hopelessly sloppy, you should look for a replacement. Also, be sure to analyze the transfers into, out of, and between your cash accounts. The amounts are often very large, and you want to be sure there are no irregularities.

I've also seen situations where bookkeepers or controllers are simply confused about how the business works, and so they post entries to the wrong accounts or projects. If you suspect that's the reason for mistakes, you might want to spend a little time explaining what's behind the numbers your controller is managing.

Why do I keep losing accountants?

"I've had to fire two part-time accountants recently. Both were highly recommended, but neither one gave me as much time and attention as we needed. Am I doing something wrong?"

Mike: Right now, good accountants are in short supply, in large part because managers are asking for better, more understandable, and more timely financial reports. If you want to recruit talented people, you should be prepared to pay market rates (or slightly above) and make sure that working for you is a positive experience. It's really that simple.

Can I refuse non-financial assignments?

"I was hired to be CFO of a venture-backed startup last year, but the CEO and the board keep dumping big projects on me that I don't feel are part of my job. (For instance, I was just put in charge of moving the company to new office space.) Although I'd like to be

cooperative, I don't even feel qualified to do some of the assignments they give me. Can I gracefully refuse?"

Mike: No, you shouldn't try to wiggle out of assignments like this. Even if it's not spelled out in your job description, a CFO typically oversees administrative areas like data processing and information technology, human resources, insurance, facilities, and various legal issues. That's particularly true in startups, where so many of the basics — policy manuals, computer systems, even office layouts — have to be developed from scratch.

But — that doesn't mean you have to handle these tasks by yourself. What the board expects (or should expect) is that you'll find appropriate experts for all these non-financial functions, and that you'll make sure these jobs are done competently and in a cost-effective way. Initially, most of your experts will probably be part-timers and outsourcers. Then, as the company grows, you can gradually bring some of these positions in-house, perhaps under a COO or other senior manager.

Should I promote my controller?

"This may be a dumb question, but does it matter if I give my controller a courtesy title of 'CFO'? Our company is pretty small, and frankly I'd rather offer a little title inflation instead of a raise."

Mike: Yes, it makes a difference. In particular, your CFO will be expected to explain the company's financial strategy to investors and lenders, which is usually not part of a controller's skill set. Putting the wrong person into the CFO position in this case will reflect badly on you, moreover, not on the person you put into that job.

Also, there's a good chance that your newly-promoted CFO will start to read salary surveys and will soon demand a paycheck that matches his title. That's often what happens with inflated titles — in the long run, they cost more than they save.

What can we do about an inept volunteer CFO?

"I'm a board member for a small non-profit group. Our CFO works on a pro bono basis, and frankly he doesn't do a very good job. We've found many mistakes in our books, checks sit around for weeks without being deposited, and his reports are incomprehensible. We'd all like to fire him – but we can't afford a paid professional, and we have no replacement candidates. Help!"

Mike: First, you want to make sure there's no evidence of fraud. The kind of sloppy bookkeeping you describe is very often associated with low-level embezzlement by a "trusted" employee (in for-profit companies as well as non-profits). Pay close attention to whether all payments actually end up in your bank account, and be sure you know the identity of every vendor who collects a check from your account.

Second, have an outside firm at least prepare your federal and state tax returns. This won't cost much, and there's a good chance your tax preparer will spot any significant problems. Remember, it's the directors of your organization who are liable for fraudulent tax returns, so you really have no choice here – regardless of the cost.

Can I pay my CFO a commission?

"I'm hoping to raise a few million dollars in venture money, and I'd like to give my CFO an incentive – say, a 2% commission on whatever he brings in. Is this ethical?"

Mike: Is it ethical? Probably. But the real question is whether your approach is a good idea. Typically, CFOs aren't paid a commission on any kind of corporate financing, debt or equity, even when they're very actively involved in negotiating the deal. If you think a financial incentive will motivate your CFO to work harder on the transaction, I'd suggest stock options instead. That way, he'll be rewarded along with the investors he helps bring into the company.

Also, you should be mindful that most investors will specifically prohibit you from paying finder's fees or commissions out of the money they contribute. They want their cash to be spent on developing and selling products, not on giving bonuses to the executive team.

Can we hire a cheaper audit firm?

"I know the conventional wisdom is that public companies absolutely must use a Big Four accounting firm, but we're getting killed by audit fees that are growing faster than our sales. Would it really affect our credibility if we used a smaller firm?"

Mike: There are some public companies — not many, though — who use mid-range or regional accounting firms for their audits. You should definitely have your audit committee solicit proposals from them, and also talk to a few clients.

But don't expect to find a bargain. In large part because of new Sarbanes- Oxley requirements, it now takes a lot more hours to conduct an audit than ever before. As you've discovered, the SOX burden is especially heavy for small public companies. Whoever you hire as an auditor may be able to suggest some cost-savings tactics. But otherwise the big fees are almost certainly going to become a fact of life for all public companies.

When Money Is Tight

"I don't want stock options I want you to pay your tab."

Who gets paid first?

"We're going through a lean period, and my partner and I disagree — very strongly, in fact — about which creditors we should pay first. I'd like to clean up all our little bills so we're not distracted by collection calls. My partner says it's better to stay in the good graces of our three biggest vendors and not worry about the small fry. Who's right?"

Mike: I think the best approach lies somewhere in between. To start with, rank your vendors by how essential they are for your operations. Payroll, taxes, utilities and health insurance will probably show up at the top of the list, because you're dead in the water if your employees walk out or the phones are shut off. Then clean up your payables list by paying the smaller accounts, especially those who provide ongoing services. Finally, speak with *all* your other vendors about your situation and payment plans. If it's too early to offer specific payment terms, at least promise to update them in a few weeks. And then make the calls on the day you promised, without fail.

How do I make a nagging creditor stop calling?

"The collections department of our former printer has been calling just about everyone in my company about our past-due account. We really don't have the cash to pay him right now, but his relentless nagging has been terrible for morale and I'd do almost anything to make him lay off. Your advice?"

Mike: Your ex-printer is no fool — he knows that if he's irritating enough, you'll find the cash to pay him, even if it's not really the right decision for your own company. Your best bet, probably, is to negotiate some kind of workout plan with him, stretching out your payments as far as possible. Then do your best to make those payments on time, so he won't have an excuse to hassle you.

The real issue, though, is that all your employees know you're having trouble paying bills. That's always bad for morale, if only because employees feel their own security is threatened. It doesn't take much imagination for them to predict a sudden layoff — and perhaps to see themselves as frustrated creditors some day. You need to clearly communicate to your employees how you plan to weather the storm and get the company back to profitability. (You might also want to open your books and show that you're getting your payables under control.) Until you've delivered on your turnaround promise, morale will continue to be a problem.

Who should I save during a layoff?

"An upcoming layoff will require me to cut 25% of my accounting department's headcount. I'm trying to figure out who to keep — people who fill the most 'indispensable' jobs or my most talented staff members. These are surprisingly different lists. Your advice?"

Mike: I'd suggest a third list, based on a purely selfish rule: If someone on your staff can't perform a necessary financial function, then you or the CFO will have to do it. That rule means you should always hang on to people with special skills or knowledge — for instance, the employees who prepare your SEC reports, translate and consolidate foreign subsidiary financials, maintain stock option records, calculate commissions (ordinarily, different for each sales person), prepare tax returns, and collect cash and manage vendor payments. These are all jobs that can take a lot of your time if you don't have the right staff, and your time is especially precious when your company is going through a rough patch.

Can we prevent a summer slump?

"Around the middle of May, our consulting volume drops by 50%-60%, because nobody wants to start a big project in the summer. Then in September business picks up again — but by then we're running on fumes. How do other companies solve this problem?"

Mike: In fact, most businesses go through seasonal cycles, not just consultants. One common solution is to offer "summer specials" — special discounts on small engagements, such as assessments and audits. If there isn't a lot of deadline pressure on your larger jobs, you might also try smoothing out your work flow during the rest of the year, by assigning fewer people to each job and stretching out the schedule. And of course you should have bank financing in place for the summer, so you're not desperate for cash by the end of the summer.

If there's absolutely no way to smooth out seasonal demand, then probably your best solution is to change your hiring practices. Tax accountants routinely hire extra staff for the big April crunch, and then drop back to a smaller core group of employees for the rest of the year. That's become an accepted practice, and it seems to work well for clients and employees alike.

What financial disasters could wreck our business?

"My company has been talking to 'disaster recovery' and 'business continuity' experts, and I notice that no one seems to pay attention to unexpected financial disasters that could cripple our business. In

your experience, what are the most important scenarios we should watch out for?"

Mike: Missing the payroll is tops on my list of financial disasters. There always seems to be a short-term cause — an investment deal that fell through, or customers who don't pay bills on time. But the real reason that most companies encounter payroll disasters is that they don't forecast their cash flow properly. That's as risky as a basement full of flammable trash. In fact, it's worse, because insurance won't cover the damage caused by a missed payroll, and the owners are likely to be personally liable for the deficiency.

Second on my list is fraud in financial reporting. This can take the form of overstated assets (phantom cash, uncollectible receivables, inventory that doesn't exist or is obsolete, purchases that are capitalized when they should be expensed) or understated liabilities and reserves (for potential expenses like intellectual property lawsuits, derivative losses, changes in foreign currency values, losses on major contracts). We've all seen how fraudulent financial reporting can devastate big public companies: The impact is usually just as serious if a smaller company is playing the same games.

Who's liable for unpaid payroll taxes?

"I just became CEO of a company that's fallen behind on paying its payroll taxes. I knew this when I was hired, and I think we can dig ourselves out. But I'm concerned about personal liability. If I pay off the oldest taxes first, my predecessor — who caused the problem — gets off the hook. But probably the only way we can afford to pay down the old taxes will be to fall behind on current tax payments for a while. Does that make me liable if the IRS shuts us down?"

Mike: Yes, you're right to be concerned — tax liabilities are a ticking time bomb that can shut down a company overnight. But don't just focus on who's liable: You need to put together a formal work-out plan with the help of your company counsel and tax advisor, and then get the plan approved by the IRS and your state tax people. Keeping everybody in the loop will almost certainly buy you more time to get current.

Crunching the Numbers

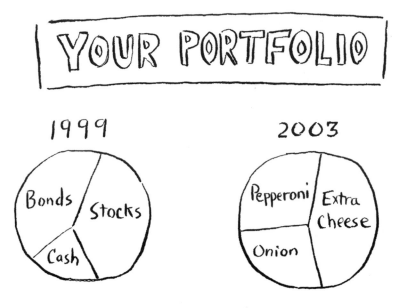

YOUR PORTFOLIO

1999

Bonds / Stocks / Cash

2003

Pepperoni / Extra Cheese / Onion

SIPRESS

What's my burn rate?

"I always thought 'burn rate' measured how much money a company was losing, and so I reported to my board that we've finally gotten our burn rate down to almost zero — meaning we're about at breakeven. One of the VCs on the board made a big stink about this; he says a company's burn rate is the total amount of cash it spends, regardless of income. Which one of us is making a fool of himself?"

Mike: You're right on this one, but it's pretty common for investors (and others) to mix up the terms "burn rate" and "monthly nut," especially in startups. A company's burn rate is the *net* amount of cash it "burns" through every month. Thus, if a company starts the year with $5 million in the bank and ends with $4 million, its burn rate is a million dollars a year. The "monthly nut" is the total amount of cash that the company spends on basic expenses — salaries, rent, travel, etc. — regardless of how much cash is actually collected.

Incidentally, one reason investors watch the monthly nut so closely is that management usually has a hard time creating trustworthy forecasts of how much cash the company will collect. It's easier to forecast and manage spending, so investors feel that at least part of the company's burn rate is under control.

How many sets of books should we keep?

"We generate a lot of revenue from pre-paid contracts, and so my controller prepares three sets of financial reports every quarter — one that shows 'actual' bookings (to show our sales performance), another that shows 'recognized' revenue, and a third that shows 'cash receipts.' He also has a fourth set of books that shows our profitability from an IRS perspective. This looks a little odd. Is he doing the right thing?"

Mike: All of these reports are legitimate, but you should decide which numbers are the best measure of your company's performance. Almost certainly, you'll choose to use traditional, accrual-based financials, which — ideally — reflect the income your company has actually earned and the liabilities you've incurred. Your controller should prepare detailed reports based on these numbers, so you can easily drill down to see why your revenues and profits might be changing. He should also prepare these reports every month — quarterly financials just aren't timely enough.

The other numbers he provides should be integrated into your regular financials in summary form. For instance, it's useful to look at bookings and taxes to understand future business trends, but you probably won't need a lot of detail unless there are big changes in these numbers. Similarly, you should see a summary of collections and receipts, but you don't need a full set of cash-based financials for this purpose.

How much detail should we show investors?

"We give our board a fairly standard balance sheet and income statement every month, but recently I was chewed out for 'hiding' a major collections problem in the accounts receivable line item. So for

our next meeting I added an appendix with details on every transaction that took place during the month. The board didn't like that approach, either. I'm really sweating about what to do for next month. Help!"

Mike: Board reporting is always a tricky problem. A good rule of thumb is to give the board a traditional big-picture view of everything that's going according to plan, and then provide more detail about specific problem areas. For example, if collections are behind plan, add a note to the balance sheet that describes three items — the difference between forecasted and actual DSO ("days sales outstanding"), an aging summary (0-30 days, 61-90 days, and 91+ days), and a list of significant problem customers. With this kind of detail, the board members should be able to see easily what's happening — and they'll probably trust you more if they feel *you* have a clear picture of the problem.

In general, you should also provide breakout detail for other major balance sheet accounts. For instance, show cash balances by bank and type of account, amounts due to major creditors (with an aging summary), inventory and inventory turns by product line, and details of any major accrued expenses. Any item that has a "material" impact on the business should be highlighted, so the board won't be caught by surprise if something blows up.

What's a credible way to figure ROI?

"My marketing people have posted a new return-on-investment calculator on our Web site that makes our value proposition look pretty convincing. However, one of my customers says our ROI numbers are 'pure fiction' (his words). How can I tell who's right?"

Mike: Most ROI calculations make the simple-minded assumption that any revenue growth or payback is a "return on investment." In reality, you should only count the net profit that an investment produces, and you should also take into account the buyer's cost of money.

Here's a simple example of what I'm talking about. Let's say you sell a $20,000 product that helps a customer generate an extra $100,000 in sales. That looks like a great payback, of course. But if the customer only nets 5% on sales (in this case, $5,000), they'll need at least four years to recover their investment. And if the buyer has also spent a few thousand dollars on interest to fund the purchase, their actual ROI is even worse. If your sales reps don't understand these numbers, they're just going to look foolish.

How can I calculate the ROI for insurance?

"Because our company has grown enormously in the last few years, I recently discovered that we should probably beef up our liability insurance. When I suggested this to the CFO, however, he reminded me that we have a rule requiring an ROI analysis for all major spending. Since the only 'return' I see for insurance is risk reduction, how would I put together the analysis he needs?"

Mike: In theory, you could run an "expected value" analysis. This would compare the cost of additional coverage to the potential loss you could incur, taking into account the statistical likelihood of a disaster and perhaps the time value of money. Of course, this kind of analysis is exactly what insurance companies do when they figure the price of a policy, so if your CFO really insists on an ROI analysis, just give him the cost of the annual premium and the dollar amount of the additional coverage you recommend.

A more useful calculation, by the way, would be to look at the economics of self-insuring your company for a larger deductible. Usually, it makes sense to buy insurance only for catastrophic events, and to set aside the savings from lower premiums to pay for incidental claims. Depending on your actual claims history, your savings from self-insurance could equal the total deductible in as little as three or four years.

Should I shoot down a bogus ROI calculation?

"I'm CFO of a company that's been talking with software vendors about a pretty major technology purchase. The IT department is enthusiastic, and I've just been asked to sign off on the deal. I don't

know about the technology, but the return on investment analysis — which the vendor calculated — is entirely bogus. In reality, the benefits are largely intangible, though everyone is so eager to get started that I doubt if my objections would stop the deal. Should I play the bad guy or just go along with the crowd?"

Mike: The real problem here is that people making decisions about capital investments don't seem to know how their own top management calculates ROI. That's a serious breakdown in communications — but this project could be a chance to teach your IT managers a more appropriate methodology. Offer to work with them to get the numbers right, so future projects won't be held up by the issues you had to raise on this contract. That way, you become an ally, not an obstacle.

You should also ask the IT management team if ROI is even an appropriate measure for this project. Sometimes companies spend money for desirable results — employee morale, brand identity, product quality — where the direct payback is hard to quantify. If ROI is your company's only measure for making an investment, worthwhile projects will probably die because you're only considering the financial benefits.

Can I trust amortization schedules?

"We've been doing a fair amount of equipment leasing lately, and it occurs to me that I've never checked the accuracy of the payment schedules that the leasing company gives us. Is this something I should worry about? And if so, how do I verify that the payments are calculated correctly?"

Mike: I just came across exactly this kind of situation recently: A software company discovered that the payment schedule provided by its leasing company called for a total of 37 monthly payments on a 36-month lease. However, this is the first time I've seen (or caught?) such an error in almost 40 years of number-crunching.

Since there are plenty of Web sites that offer free amortization calculators, it's easy to double-check a simple debt repayment schedule.

Leases are a little more complicated, especially if the leasing company is reluctant to disclose its interest rates and fees. If you can pry those numbers out of the lessor, you can easily duplicate the payment schedule in a spreadsheet and compare the results. Otherwise, if the numbers are secret — well, there's not much you can do except trust the leasing company.

How do we verify the accuracy of accounting software?

"Our auditors say Sarbanes-Oxley requires us to certify that our accounting software is accurate and mistake-free, which makes sense in theory. But we have no way to inspect or test the vendor's code — the software could be skimming off a little cash here and there, and we'd never know. So how can we certify the integrity of the software?"

Mike: Sarbanes-Oxley has brought this issue to the forefront, but the issue has been around for a long time. Before you install any new financial program you must do "due diligence" to ensure the software is accurate and appropriate for your business. The two most significant steps are confirming with other users that the software functions as claimed, and operating the software with test data before converting to the new system.

Many companies will process transactions for a period (say, one month) in parallel, using both their current software and the new software. At the end of the trial period, you should compare the results and make sure you get *exactly* the same numbers. Ideally, you should pick a test period that gives the software a full workout — for instance, a year-end closing or perhaps a conversion of international sales. And keep an eye on the company's tech support bulletin board to see if there are bug reports or other issues you should watch out for.

How do I figure interest rates on leases?

"Now that interest rates are so low, I'm thinking about buying out the leases on a lot of our leased equipment. But when I go through

the lease documents, I can't seem to find our actual interest rate quoted anywhere. How can I compare my financing options?"

Mike: Leasing companies hate to disclose interest rates for an obvious reason—their rates are almost always far higher than most other financing options. Even if you know the interest rate on your leases, however, your buy-vs.-lease analysis should also take into account the tax impact, the actual buyout price, and even equipment servicing costs (which may be bundled with your lease).

In the end, however, you'll almost certainly find that buying out your leases is a no-brainer. Interest rates have dropped so much lately that any long-term financing arrangements you made a few years ago are now likely to carry a price tag far above current market rates.

Payroll Perils

"Of course, with the position that has the benefits – medical, dental, et cetera – there is no salary."

How should we interpret salary survey data?

"I'm on my board's compensation committee, and we look at several salary surveys when we set executive salaries. However, the best surveys break out their numbers according to geography, company revenues, headcount, etc. Any thoughts on which of these factors is most important?"

Mike: You probably won't find this data in salary surveys, but I've found that the single most important factor in executive pay is the development stage of the company – pre-funding, venture-backed, profitable, post-IPO, etc. As a rule, the more mature the company, the higher the pay.

Of course, company maturity usually corresponds with revenue level. But not always: You should expect to pay a lot more to recruit a CEO for a $10 million public company than you would for someone to run a private company with similar revenues.

How does phantom stock work?

"Some of my employees have been lobbying for stock in my company, since it's likely that we'll be acquired in the next two or three years. I'm a little confused about whether to give them common stock, options, or 'phantom' stock (whatever that is). Your advice?"

Mike: Phantom stock is by far the simplest and most flexible approach, especially if your goal is to reward employees when the company is sold. Basically, phantom or "shadow" stock is a promise to give employees a pre-determined share of equity appreciation when a "change of control" transaction takes place. The paperwork is very simple, and you don't end up with a bunch of minority shareholders. From the employee's perspective, moreover, there are no tax issues until the sale actually takes place.

The one issue that's a little tricky is figuring out a realistic base-line valuation for the phantom shares you give out. Since your goal is to reward key people for any *increase* in the company's value, you'll be over-rewarding them if you set the phantom stock valuation too low and under-rewarding them if it's too high.

Do I have to pay severance pay?

"I just fired a long-term employee for what I'll only describe as 'sleazy behavior.' Ordinarily, we give departing employees a generous severance package, but severance is not mentioned in our employee handbook and I don't feel at all generous toward this guy. Do I have to pay anything?"

Mike: If you've paid severance to absolutely every other employee you've fired or laid off, your prior actions probably give your ex-employee a legal basis for a claim, regardless of what your employee handbook says. You're in a much stronger bargaining position if you can show that you've paid severance only some of the time—for instance only to employees who were laid off because of lack of work, not for poor performance.

You might also try to establish that you suffered cash losses due to your ex-employee's "sleazy" behavior. That way, you'll have a reasonable counter-claim if you have to negotiate a settlement or even go to court.

Should I offer a declining bonus?

"I have three developers working on an upgrade that's really essential. I promised them a huge bonus if they met their deadline, but it looks like they won't even come close. Now I'm afraid they have no incentive to keep pushing. My controller has suggested that we keep the bonus but deduct 10% for every week the project slips. Do you think this will work?"

Mike: There are some employees, like sales reps, who are strongly motivated by cash incentives. Unfortunately, developers mostly fall at the opposite end of the incentive spectrum. They certainly won't complain if you offer them a bonus, but—as you've discovered—they won't work extra hard to catch the brass ring.

The trouble with the kind of bonus arrangement you set up, moreover, is that it turns into a disincentive the moment the target date has been missed. Your controller's suggestion makes the problem worse: Your developers will probably see this plan as a diabolical form of pay reduction, not as a reward, and they'll react accordingly. You're probably better off promising a partial bonus—say, 50%—whenever the project is finally finished.

In the future, I'd suggest you skip the bonuses and focus on getting realistic forecasts of development time. Be prepared to cut features if the schedule runs too long—for developers who take pride in their work, that's often a more powerful incentive than cash payments.

Do I really owe the IRS money?

"Ouch! I signed up last year with a small payroll service, and I just leaned that they've gone bankrupt without handing over the last two

quarters of payroll taxes to the IRS. Now the IRS claims I still owe the taxes. Do I really?"

Mike: Sadly, yes. The IRS will probably let you off the hook on late-payment penalties, but from their perspective the taxes were never paid. End of discussion.

For what it's worth, it's tough to protect yourself from his kind of situation. The IRS doesn't let employers verify the status of payroll tax accounts electronically, so you have to request a written transcript of your quarterly 941 account from the IRS every time you want to verify that your taxes have been credited properly. Naturally, not many people go through this hassle. The best method is to rely on payroll services that you know are adequately capitalized — preferably public companies like ADP and Paychex, whose financial information is easily available.

How should we accrue vacation pay?

"We've been insanely busy for the past few years, and most of my people are now owed a ton of vacation time — equal to more than 12% of our annual payroll. Since this is a very real liability, I think it belongs on the balance sheet. But my controller says we can't accrue unpaid salary liabilities for more than three months without paying them. A second opinion, please?"

Mike: This is one of those times when tax accounting and financial accounting don't follow the same rules. The IRS doesn't want you to accrue long-term payroll obligations, such as bonuses and vacation time, and so they insist on payment within 90 days of the end of your fiscal year if you want to keep the deduction in that year. According to financial accounting rules, however, you should show all vested vacation liabilities on your balance sheet because they're as real as any other payable or debt.

Incidentally, you might want to rewrite your vacation policy to put a cap on how much time an employee can accrue — a so-called "use it or lose it" policy. Especially if you go through a significant round of layoffs, you can be hit with some very painful cash outlays whenever employees leave with accrued vacation time.

Should we give our part-timers a raise?

"We have several part-time employees who are paid the same hourly rates as our regular staff. The part-timers are now lobbying for a higher rate, saying that they're more productive (that's true — they waste less time on meetings and socializing) and don't get benefits. Your advice?"

Mike: All other factors being equal, I've always felt that full-time staff people deserve a pay premium because they demonstrate more commitment than part-timers do. Commitment can take many forms — putting in a few extra hours, thinking up new ideas or solving problems when you're in the shower, or perhaps defending the company's reputation when something goes wrong. Extra pay is a way of recognizing that your company values this kind of commitment.

At the same time, you don't want to under-pay your part-time staff. Part-timers are naturally sensitive to market rates in compensation, and the best-qualified may jump ship if you're paying below-market wages. Make sure you have a target compensation level for part-timers (say, 90%, or 100%, or 110% of prevailing hourly rates) and adjust your pay levels accordingly.

Should my developers pay out-of-state taxes?

"When we install software, my developers typically spend a couple of weeks at the customer's site, living in a hotel. Now my accountant tells me that these developers will have to file income tax returns in every state they've worked, just like high-paid athletes who pay state taxes based on the number of away games they play in each state. Nobody else I know does this. Is my accountant crazy?"

Mike: Unfortunately, your accountant knows what he's talking about. State governments are trying to tax everything in sight (I've heard that California is even trying to tax satellites whenever they fly over the state). Worse, the rules vary from state to state, so there are no general guidelines you can rely on to untangle the mess.

In your case, your training and consulting employees are clearly spending a significant part of their time working out of state, so you should withhold and report payroll taxes for at least this group of employees at the individual state level. (Of course, they'll have to file their own state tax returns for each of these states, which won't make them happy.) If you're not already outsourcing your payroll processing, it probably makes sense for you to give this task to one of the big national firms — they're good at staying up to date on all the rules.

How should we set partnership salaries?

"I'm one of three partners who set up a company that's become very profitable. We each put in equal working capital, and we've each taken the same small salary for the past three years. But now my two partners, who mostly handle sales, are lobbying for big raises based on 'market comparables.' That leaves me holding the short end of the stick, because I'm the inside guy who handles operations and finance stuff — which usually isn't as highly paid as sales. What do you think is fair here?"

Mike: As you've no doubt figured out, partnership pay is a subject you should always wrestle with *before* you go into business with anyone else. Yes, it's an academic question then, but once you're fighting over real money the issues get far more emotional.

But even if you're already making money, there are bound to be good years and less-good years, so you need to define an ongoing formula that all three partners accept (perhaps with some grumbling). I'd start by making a distinction between how you split the profits your company earns and how you pay yourselves for your day-to-day work. It's reasonable to peg your individual salaries to market standards, since that's usually a fair measure of the skills and effort a job requires. Then come up with a separate formula for dividing corporate profits. For instance, you could agree to split all profits equally, since you each contributed the same working capital. Or you could devise a formula that puts extra weight on certain high-value contributions. I know one group, for example, that gives two rainmaker partners a 25% bonus share of profits because winning new clients is the lifeblood of their business.

Incidentally, I wouldn't take for granted that an "inside" partner automatically gets paid at the bottom end of the totem pole. In businesses with tight margins, a manager who's a whiz at operations often contributes more net profit than any of the sales folk.

The Chain of Command

D. Fradin

Should I respect the chain of command?

"I'm a consultant working on a small M&A project for an investor who owns a piece of a young company. I've discovered a scary lack of financial controls, though probably no fraud (yet). I think I should alert the board of directors, but my partner thinks I should talk to the CFO first. Your advice?"

Mike: Give the CFO first crack at the problem. If he makes excuses or doesn't demonstrate a sense of urgency, immediately escalate to the CEO. The action the CEO should take is to put the issue of controls on the agenda of the next board meeting, along with a specific action plan. If that doesn't happen, go directly to the head of the board's audit committee.

Bear in mind that poor financial controls are almost always a sign of a weak CFO, and a weak CFO usually means the CEO and the board aren't doing their jobs. Even if the board takes action on tougher controls, the ultimate solution might be to replace the CFO. Be prepared for some nasty political battles.

Who's my boss?

"I'm the CFO of a company that's under a lot of stress lately, and there's an ugly dispute between the CEO and a chairman who owns about half the company. I'm caught in the middle: The CEO tells me to do things that the chairman immediately countermands. Who should I listen to?"

Mike: In fact, you're not caught in the middle at all. As a CFO, you report directly to the CEO, not to anyone else. If you're convinced the CEO is acting improperly, you should report your concerns to the board of directors. But even then, you're expected to discuss the problem first with the CEO.

And that's what you should do with your current situation: Start by asking your CEO to resolve his problems with the company's chairman, and point out that the conflict is making your job impossible. If he refuses to take action, then you have a legitimate issue to take to the board. (By the way, I'll bet the board members know what's going on and plan to replace the CEO.)

How can I safely delegate setting up a new business?

"This is my first time starting a company, and I'm being overwhelmed with trivia — setting up checking accounts, finding office space, getting credit card merchant accounts, even renting a stupid postage meter. I tried delegating this stuff, but the people I appointed either dumped the tough decisions in my lap or they got snookered by slimy sales people. What can I do?"

Mike: It's very common for entrepreneurs to feel that day-to-day administration of the business is a waste of their time — until there's a problem. In fact, you should be involved in the final decisions about setting up your office systems (yes, even the mail room). Investing a day or two of your time up front will help make sure that everything runs smoothly once the business is operating at full speed.

This is also a good chance to define your management style for your employees. Chances are, they haven't yet figured out what you want, so they're unsure where you'd draw the line with salespeople and leave too many decisions for you to make. For instance, have you clearly described what kind of office space you're looking for? If not, don't be surprised when the people you ask to check out possible space bring you bad choices. Use these startup decisions to shape your new company style, and pretty soon your employees will be eager to handle the day-to-day details for you.

Who should sign checks?

"This is going to sound like a trivial question, but is there a good rule of thumb about who should sign company checks? Our founder insists on signing every check over $100, and he wants a second signature (the CFO's) on any payment over $2,500. We're always interrupting him to get checks signed, and sometimes dozens of checks get 'lost' on his desk for weeks at a time. It's a real nuisance."

Mike: Yes, I've seen this kind of obsession with detail in many growing companies. The CEO complains that he's being constantly interrupted, but he still wants to sign every check, proofread every letter, and sign off on every project spec. My usual suggestion—which most CEOs seem happy to accept—is that they reverse the check-signing process: The CFO signs all checks less than, say, $5,000, and the CEO is the required second signer on all checks over that amount. If the CEO is still nervous, you can give him a simple weekly report of all the checks that you signed, so he knows where the company's money is going.

It's also helpful to prepare a list of the checks you issued last month, sorted in ascending order. That will easily show how many small checks your CEO signed and the dollars these checks represented as a percentage of total spending. Chances are, you'll see an 80%/20% pattern (Pareto's Law)—that is, 80% of the checks you issue probably add up to not much more than 20% of your total payments. If your CEO signs just the big checks, he'll be able to watch the company's outlays almost as effectively as he would by signing all checks.

How do I deal with a know-it-all boss?

"I took a job six months ago as controller of a $5 million electronics company. I've since discovered that the CEO thinks he's an accounting expert and second-guesses everything I do (he does the same to our outside accountant and tax guy). His opinions are mostly in the ballpark, but sometimes he's way, way wrong. How can I get him to butt out?"

Mike: The fact that he cares about accounting issues is a blessing—far too many CEOs think financial reports are black magic and don't even try to understand what the numbers mean. If your boss is trying to make sure transactions are recorded properly and wants accounts set up in a way that provides better management guidance, that's certainly a reasonable request. And remember, it's his company.

Of course, if his instructions involve fraud—for instance, overstating revenues or understating expenses—you should stick to your guns and even be prepared to quit your job, because you must never be a party to incorrect financial statements. But my experience is that most accounting disputes reflect honest misunderstandings of balance sheets and other accounting reports. If you can gracefully help your CEO understand these issues, you'll both be a lot happier.

Keeping an Eye on the Cash

"Oh, __that__ three billion dollars."

What's the rule for keeping a cash reserve?

"Is there a good rule of thumb for how much cash a small company should keep on hand? My partner says he heard that we should have a reserve of one month's worth of sales. Is that the right number?"

Mike: Nope, it's not that simple. First of all, you should always measure your cash balance against your cash expenses, not your revenues. In particular, you should focus on expenses you absolutely can't defer even for a month or two—usually, payroll and payments to key vendors (who may already insist on COD terms). The only meaningful "rule of thumb" is that you should have enough cash on hand so that the survival of the business is never at risk. Period.

The answer also depends on how reliable your cash flow is, and how easily you can raise money to solve a shortfall (for example, by borrowing against a credit line or collecting your receivables more aggressively). I've seen businesses operate with skimpy amounts of cash in the bank because they have lots of customers and money comes in every day. At the other extreme, there are companies that rely on big, hard-to-predict payments from a few big clients, so a huge cash cushion — ideally, six months worth of expenses — is essential.

How do we manage fluctuating cash balances?

"One of my board members always complains that we don't have the 'right amount' of cash on hand. Either the cash balance is too high and we're not investing enough, or it's too low and we're living dangerously. The truth is, I don't have a lot of control over this number: We generate a lot of cash from event promotion, so we're flush just before an event and then we go for a couple of months without seeing much revenue (we also don't have many expenses in the slow periods, however). What can I tell this guy to get him off my back?"

Mike: Your director's complaint is a common one, especially if he hasn't managed cash in a dynamic situation. His real concern, I suspect, is that he can't make an informed judgment about the company's risk of running out of cash. There are few events that cause as much damage as being unable to meet payroll, pay taxes, etc., and it's entirely appropriate for a director to worry about such things.

To deal with his concerns, I suggest you put together three graphs every month. The first graph shows collections, spending, and the cash balance, by month. The second graph shows how many months of upcoming operating expenses you can cover with the cash you have at the end of each month. You can use these two graphs to explain (1) the rationale in the changes in the cash balance, as well as (2) the risk associated with these changes (fewer months of cash on hand indicates higher risk). If your forecast indicates light spending for the next few months, for example, it's safe for you to have a relatively low cash balance at the end of the current month.

I'd also add a third graph that would show the sensitivity of changes in the assumptions that underlie your forecast. If customer payments don't come in when you expect or you get hit with an unplanned expense, will you have enough cash in the bank to protect yourself? Very few managers can answer this question, and your unhappy director almost certainly will be impressed by your cash-management skills.

How aggressive should I be with invested cash?

"We have $2 million that we raised for a big product launch next year. Right now it's sitting in a money market fund, earning almost no interest. I'd like to see if we can get a higher rate of return for at least some of our cash — after all, it seems to me that the people who gave us this money were risk-takers themselves. Are there any accounting rules about how we're supposed to handle our reserves?"

Mike: The basic accounting principle is that you never, ever want to write down the value of assets on your watch. Even shopping around for an extra point or two of interest can sometimes be risky: Before the big S&L crash a few years back, CFOs routinely parked "excess" cash in small-town banks that were hungry for deposits — and several companies lost millions of dollars when these banks went under. Your job is to protect the company's cash, not to dabble in derivatives, currency futures, or other high-risk games.

(If you genuinely think your company's investors feel differently, you should ask them to formally approve a more aggressive investment strategy. My guess is that they won't want any more risk exposure than they already have.)

What should we do with a windfall?

"My company had a bang-up year, and now we have almost $250,000 in cash sitting in the bank. My partners (five of us) can't agree on what to do with the money. Two partners want to issue a dividend, and three of us want to reinvest it in growing the business so we can generate even more profits like this in the future. How would you resolve this debate?"

Mike: You should probably treat this as an exercise in forecasting. Just saying you want to "invest in growing the business" doesn't mean much — you need to make a careful prediction about the future value of your $250,000 compared to its net present value as a dividend. Obviously, even the best forecast involves some guesswork, so you should also take risk factors into account. But if you can get your partners to agree on your forecast assumptions, chances are the debate will be much easier to resolve.

Remember also that one of your partners may have a pressing personal need for cash — say, for college tuition bills. If that's the case, the same calculation may show that he's better off borrowing money than collecting a cash dividend.

How can I prevent repayment of company debt?

"I'm about to make an angel investment in a one-person company that looks very promising. The one hitch: The company has borrowed almost $100,000, mostly from the founder and his family. I'd be okay with paying this money back when and if we sell the company. But I definitely don't want my investment to go toward debt repayment, and I'm not even happy with paying it back out of operating revenues. Any ideas?"

Mike: There's nothing unusual about what you want — investors always expect that their money will fund specific, future programs (such as finishing product development or ramping up a marketing effort), not pay for "prior sins." The approach you suggest — wait until a liquidity event to repay debts to the founder and his family — is a good solution and is not unusual as part of closing a financing deal. You might also point out to the founder that leaving a big chunk of debt on a startup's balance sheet has a negative impact on valuation and the company's ability to borrow from banks, so he may be better off converting the debt to equity.

Can I pay bills of Company A with cash from Company B?

"I set up a new company recently, and I'd like to pay its bills out of my old company's checking account, which has lots of money. However, my accountant insists I have to take out the cash as profit,

pay taxes on it, and then invest it in the new business. Why?"

Mike: Your accountant is right in principle: You can't deduct one company's expenses on another company's tax return. If the companies are independent (and they should be), their financial and tax reporting should never be mixed together. However, a much simpler approach would be to have your profitable company *lend* the new company money to pay its bills. As long as both companies treat the payments as loans, the expenses will show up on the right set of financial statements and you'll pay the correct amount of taxes.

Who should take the risk on exchange rates?

"We sell software through about a dozen resellers overseas, and last year we implemented one 'world price' — everything sells for the same price in dollars, regardless of fluctuations in local exchange rates. Now our resellers are complaining their margins get hammered whenever the exchange rate is unfavorable. I see their point, but I don't want to absorb currency losses myself. Advice?"

Mike: In the end, someone has to assume the risk of currency fluctuations. Regardless of what your contracts say, my experience has been that resellers will book a payable to you in their local currency at the time they inventory the software. And that's the maximum they'll ever agree to pay you—if you're lucky.

Of course, you increase your exposure dramatically if your resellers can't afford to pay you until they collect from their own customers. I saw one company that had significant sales to a Hong Kong distributor, who then resold the product to customers throughout South Korea, China, the Phillipines and Malaysia. There were dramatic declines in the value of the local currencies, the distributor had trouble collecting the Hong Kong dollars, and the U.S. parent wound up writing off about 40% of its receivables. You might be able to protect yourself by taking option positions in especially volatile foreign currencies, but the best hedge against risks is to insist on prompt payments.

Where the Money Comes From

"By God, gentlemen, I believe we've found it — the Fountain of Funding!"

How do I know if customers are profitable?

"We have two or three very big customers who pay rock-bottom prices, and I suspect we're actually losing money on their business. However, my sales people insist these accounts 'pay for our overhead' and they point out that fixed costs like rent and payroll wouldn't go down much if we got rid of these customers. Is there a simple way to measure customer profitability?"

Mike: Sure. Most accounting systems will let you set up separate profit-and-loss reports for each project or customer, which show you how much gross profit (revenues minus direct costs) you're earning on each account. If the numbers show that there's no profit from an individual customer, that account is obviously not making any contribution toward your overhead—no matter what your sales people believe.

Once you're collecting data on customer-level profitability, incidentally, you might want to start paying sales commissions on gross profit rather than gross revenues. Right now, your sales folk have an incentive to keep cutting prices to win big deals, even if you lose money on those deals. That's a bad situation.

Can a client refuse to pay a cost overrun?

"I quoted a new client a $10,000 fee for redesigning their Web site, and I thought I made it clear that the price was an 'estimate.' The actual job came in at $14,100, based on my hourly rate. Now the client says he thought I was quoting a fixed price, and he refuses to budge on paying for the extra hours. Can he do this?"

Mike: Sorry, but you really have no recourse here. Any time you get a new client, you should be absolutely clear what the fee arrangements are. You don't always need a formal contract, but it's best to put the terms in writing—a simple letter is often enough. Since you didn't do this, you assumed the risk of cost overruns (as well as the potential benefit of getting the job done for less), and should be prepared to live with the $10,000 fee.

It's also a good practice on complex hourly-rate projects to keep track of whether the job is "on plan" or not. As soon as you see a potential cost overrun, even a small one, bring it to the client's attention. It's better to let your client decide whether to scale back the project or proceed with realistic expectations of higher costs. Surprising a client with a 40% last-minute extra charge is guaranteed to create bad feelings.

Should I let a client run a tab?

"One of my clients has asked me to convert last quarter's invoice into an interest-bearing note at 2%/month until his new business begins generating revenue. I'd like to be supportive, and I can afford to park the money—especially at 24% a year. He's even promised to pay me before he takes a salary. Should I help out?"

Mike: This is a little like investing in junk bonds: a high rate of interest, with an above-average risk of default. Yes, you can afford to defer collection—but can you afford to write off the whole amount if the client fails? Would an investor put the same money at risk in return for a 24% interest rate? Do you trust the client's financial projections? These are questions you should ask yourself before committing to the deal.

If you decide to go ahead (or don't have a choice), there are several ways you might make the arrangement more attractive. You can ask for an equity kicker — essentially, stock options. You can also request a personal guarantee from the owner. And you can negotiate better terms, perhaps even COD payment, for future sales. If you don't make the deal at least a little painful for your client, the next time he's short of cash you'll almost certainly get an invitation to make an even larger "investment."

What can I do about a slow-paying customer?

"We have a major customer whose payments are always in arrears by about four months. Every month, he pays the oldest invoice and then runs up roughly the same amount in new charges. I've talked with him about the situation, and his attitude is basically, 'That's the way I do business. If you don't like it, I'll find someone else who will.' However, if he leaves, I'm afraid we'll have to spend a lot of money on lawyers and collection agents to get any of the old balance. Suggestions?"

Mike: Of course, you're being abused — and by a customer who doesn't even pretend to be a good guy. I could point out that you're partly at fault for not dealing promptly with past-due accounts. But you've probably figured that out already.

If you set aside your feelings, however, the simple question is: How profitable is the forced "investment" you've made in this customer? Right now, most companies are paying interest rates in the 5%-10% range, so — unless your margins are terrible — it's likely that you're still making a reasonable profit on the customer's business. The money you tie up in receivables is like any other capital expenditure: Sometimes the investment is highly profitable, and sometimes it's less than great.

If you do decide to get tough with this customer, the good news is that he's been paying your bills regularly, so he'll have a hard time claiming that your performance was unsatisfactory. To strengthen your case, you should quietly start building a paper trail — get signatures when you deliver anything, make a record of every phone conversation (including tech support and customer service calls), and make sure there are no ambiguities in your invoices and statements.

Can we be considered a preferred creditor?

"Our biggest reseller is having financial problems. They normally pay us within 45-60 days, but they've offered COD terms until they straighten out their cash problems. I thought that would protect us, but my CFO says we might have to give the money back if they go bankrupt. Is he right?"

Mike: You're walking a fine line here, but bankruptcy courts have generally approved COD terms for *current* sales, especially when the customer's business is likely to fail if key vendors refuse to deliver essential goods and services. Be sure to document your COD agreement and keep meticulous records.

However, the preferences rule definitely does apply to your older unpaid invoices, which the courts won't let your customer pay ahead of other creditors. This is a matter of basic fairness: The courts want to make sure all creditors get their pro-rated share of any remaining assets, so anyone who gets preferential treatment usually has to return the money to the asset pool.

Should we 'lend' money to bid on a big deal?

"There's a very large company in our industry that we'd love to have as a customer, but I'm wondering if their terms are legitimate. They insist we'll have to give them 60 days to pay our invoices, which is okay — but they also want us to 'lend' them $250,000 up front, which they'll refund when they pay for the components we sell them. As you can imagine, we've had some pretty noisy debates about this deal. Your advice?"

Mike: This kind of "prebate" is a common practice in some commodity industries — for example, semiconductors — so your prospective customer isn't making an illegitimate request. Of course, you'll want to take special care in evaluating the customer's creditworthiness, since a default would be extra-expensive.

The harder question is whether the deal makes sense for you financially. The $250,000 upfront payment doesn't guarantee that you'll get any orders — it just gives you "preferred vendor" status and the right to bid against other vendors. You'll need to take in account the cost of the working capital you tie up in this deal, and the tight margins you'll have to accept to compete effectively. Unless you're running a very lean, high volume operation, this deal could be quite unprofitable.

How should we structure an OEM license?

"We have a chance to license one of our software tools to a company that will embed it in their own product. My lawyer has been great about identifying all the little points we have to negotiate about royalties, customization, support, etc. But he admits he's not sure which issues deserve the most attention and which ones are probably unimportant. Are there two or three critical success factors you feel we should focus on?"

Mike: It's interesting that you feel royalties and support are "little points," because in my experience these are the two areas where you're most likely to run into surprise situations. It's pretty easy to draft a contract that covers all the issues on the day a deal is signed, but the software world changes so fast that your relationship with the buyer could be very different even a few years from now.

With a software license, I'd also be extra careful to spell out how the code will be modified and upgraded in the future. Will you control these changes or will maintenance be taken over by your licensee — or even by the licensee's own customers? That's an especially important point if your software will end up in a "mission-critical" application where users are ultra-sensitive about bugs or sluggish performance. If you've handed over code maintenance to a licensee, they should assume responsibility for its performance.

How can we minimize contract changes?

"We have a standard contract when we sell software, but our customers routinely tinker with the terms. It's never anything substantial, but the endless legal reviews cost us a lot of money, and it's a huge hassle trying to keep track of special pricing, oddball deadlines, and other non-standard terms. Does everyone have this problem?"

Mike: If there are terms that always seem to cause problems, it might be easier to change your standard language to reflect the kinds of changes that customers usually request. Even better, borrow boilerplate language from any large vendor whose contracts have already passed muster by your prospective customers. If you can say, 'You accepted this identical clause when you signed a contract with Oracle,' you make it a little harder for a customer to demand changes.

Ultimately, though, customers call the shots on contracts unless you're in an extremely powerful position and are willing to walk away from big sales. One CFO I know offered a "clean contract" bonus to any sales rep who negotiated a no-changes deal. It was a nice idea, but no one ever earned the bonus.

The Care & Feeding of Sales Reps

Can I recover a draw against commissions?

"I have a sales rep who just hasn't been able to close any business in the past nine months. It's not entirely his fault (in fact, he used to be pretty good), but I've decided to fire him. Trouble is, he owes the company almost $50,000 for advances against commissions. Can I at least deduct this from his severance pay?"

Mike: No one in sales will love this answer, but here it is: A draw against commissions is simply a loan to an employee and should be paid back like any other loan. Period. In fact, by not trying to collect an over-extended draw, you're sending a message to everyone on your sales team that there's no penalty for poor results. Is that what you want them to think?

Of course, your terminated sales rep is likely to hire a lawyer, who'll argue that a draw doesn't need to be paid back. Before that happens, you might want to negotiate a smaller payback amount in return for a written loan agreement with your ex-employee. And you should review your employee handbook and hiring letters to make sure they specify that draws are always "recoverable."

Is a commission override reasonable?

"We're talking to a potential vice president of sales who plans to spend half his time on selling and the other half on building a sales organization for us. The problem is commissions: He argues that his earnings will suffer if he spends a lot of time on management work, so he feels he should get a commission override for sales brought in by the people he hires. That could scale up to more money than we want to spend.Advice?"

Mike: Sales folks often come up with remarkably ingenious reasons why they should be paid high commissions. Your sales VP's theory, however, is way over the top: He's expecting to earn commissions even for time he spends *not* selling. You should point out to him that building the sales machine is part of his job description as a vice president, and if he can't handle the management side of the job he shouldn't be a candidate for a VP slot.

Naturally, I presume that you've offered him a compensation package that's based on realistic market rates. If not, then you should bump up either his commission rate or his base pay until it's competitive.

Is there a good incentive for selling services?

"I'd like to get my sales people to sell more maintenance contracts and professional services, but they say it's easier and more lucrative for them to sell product licenses. I'm reluctant to increase the commission rate – that's a slippery slope – but I can't think of any other approach. Have you seen a good solution?"

Mike: Even if you double the commission on services (which some companies have tried), your reps will still put most of their efforts into closing big-ticket product deals that they know will result in the fattest commission checks. One approach is to bundle your services and software together –

for instance, by requiring customers to buy maintenance the first year, or by including installation in the basic product price. Or else you can set two separate sales quotas, one for product sales and a second for services. If a rep doesn't meet both quotas, you might hold back the annual trip to Hawaii or part of their year-end bonus.

You might also look at setting up two distinct sales groups, each with their own comp plan. I've seen this strategy in several companies, and it seems to work well.

How should we handle commissions on refunds?

"We recently had to refund a customer's money on a pretty hefty sale, frankly because our engineers promised something they couldn't deliver. Now the sales guy who handled the account is arguing that he should be allowed to keep his commission, since he acted in good faith and put in at least two months of hard work on this deal. I'd like to find a way to compensate him – but my CFO insists it would set a 'terrible' precedent. Your vote?"

Mike: Your CFO is right – you should compensate sales people for sales, not for situations where your products are returned and you wind up giving back the cash. By not paying a commission on this deal, moreover, you're sending a message that sales reps should take a tough "show me" attitude toward the development team's promises. That kind of pressure will ultimately produce better products and more reliable forecasts.

In the short term, however, you also have an unhappy sales rep who feels his company isn't treating him fairly. To keep him productive, you may want to give him a special one-time bonus – but be clear that it's not a commission, and it won't be paid again if a similar problem occurs in the future.

How about deals where the customer can back out?

"My company does custom engineering, usually on year-long projects. To help sell these projects, we recently changed our contracts to let clients cancel at the end of a phase without penalty

(no one ever does, but they appreciate the flexibility). But now my CFO says we should only pay commissions for the current phase of a project, which is bound to annoy the sales guys. Is he right?"

Mike: Well, your CFO does have a good point: You shouldn't give your sales folk full credit today for projects that might be cancelled — or, perhaps more likely, scaled back — at some future date. Your sales reps should always have a stake in making sure clients are satisfied.

However, delaying commissions when there's little risk of cancellation isn't a great solution. Your sales reps will be annoyed, and they'll probably try to convince clients to sign iron-clad contracts instead of taking advantage of your new flexible approach. Rather than delay payment, you might adjust your commission agreements to say that if a client cancels a later phase, any advance commissions are either recoverable or will be credited against other deals.

What's the hidden cost of extended payment terms?

"My VP of sales has been cutting big deals lately that give customers a six-month grace period for paying invoices. His argument is that we're better off waiting a while to get paid full price instead of giving buyers a discount for net 30 day terms. I get the logic of what he says, but somehow I know there's a hidden tradeoff. What am I missing?"

Mike: The tradeoff is the cost of the working capital or loans you need to cover payroll and other overhead while you wait to collect from slow-paying clients. If you have plenty of cash, waiting six months to collect on a full-price sale probably costs you about as much as giving a 5%-10% discount for immediate payment. Both are very expensive solutions when you work out an equivalent annual interest rate.

If you don't have much cash, your sales guy's logic doesn't work at all. Sooner or later, you'll have so much money tied up in receivables that you'll have trouble meeting payroll and other expenses. Then you'll probably have to give up a big chunk of equity to get the cash you need.

Looking Backwards: Benchmarks & Metrics

SIPRESS

"You say it's win-win, but what if you're wrong-wrong and it all goes bad-bad?"

How should we set up our cost categories?

"Is there some accounting rule that says I have to set up my cost accounting categories in a particular way? I'd like to mirror our internal budget categories — for instance, R&D and Support are in the same department, and my salary as CEO should probably go into Sales, since that's where I spend 90% of my time. But my bookkeeper argues that we should follow 'standard industry practice,' whatever that is. Why?"

Mike: That's a fair question. Your financial statements should be set up so that they help management understand how the business is operating, but you also want costs grouped so that you can benchmark them against other companies in your industry. If you set up unusual categories, a lot of people — including investors, bankers, tax advisors, and eventually potential acquirers — won't be sure they can trust your numbers.

You'll also find that traditional financial reporting categories can be pretty flexible about reflecting your actual business operations. The toughest challenge, especially for companies with fewer than 20 or so employees, is to match up employees with cost centers. I've found it's usually best to allocate an individual's salary and related costs to a single cost center, even though he or she may work for several departments. Splitting an employee's time among multiple cost centers may seem logical, but eventually the allocation formula becomes outdated and arbitrary.

How do public companies report their G&A costs?

"I've been benchmarking our G&A costs — including rent, admin and finance salaries, the phone system, and the IT group — against the G&A numbers that public software companies publish. But a friend warned me that many public companies now allocate at least part of these costs to operating groups like sales and R&D, which would produce much lower G&A numbers. Is this true?"

Mike: Your friend is correct. Generally, public companies allocate costs to other functional areas whenever they can divide up those costs reasonably.

For instance, it's common to allocate facility costs to groups like sales, marketing, customers support, manufacturing, etc., on the basis of square footage or number of employees in each department. If a cost can't be divided up — the CEO's salary, say, or the expense of preparing the annual report — then it's more likely to end up in the corporate G&A line item. But there's no easy way to tell how each company handles its allocation formulas, so company-to-company benchmarking is always an inexact science.

What does a high payables ratio indicate?

"I've always looked at a potential client's Days Payables Outstanding (DPO) ratio as an indication of how fast the company pays its bills. But the CFO of a public company I work with insists this isn't always true. His DPO is high, he says, because his company hires outsourcers for a lot of work that other companies

handle with in-house employees whose cost doesn't show up as a payable. Is he right?"

Mike: He's absolutely right. The DPO ratio—accounts payable divided by one month's cash expenses—is occasionally interesting to investors, because it shows how much working capital has been supplied by trade creditors (usually without any interest payments). But the DPO ratio is almost useless if you're trying to calculate whether you'll get paid on time. You're better off checking with traditional credit-monitoring services like D&B or contacting a few other vendors who do business with your prospective clients.

What are the right metrics for services?

"We have three senior networking engineers who do installation and customization work for our clients at a rate of $1,600 a day. They're always busy, and yet somehow we barely break even on their department. If I knew what to measure, I'm sure I could figure out a solution — but nobody here can agree on metrics for professional services. Can you help?"

Mike: The two metrics you should watch most closely are average billing rate and productivity (i.e., percent of time billed). Your current $1,600 billing rate is reasonable, so you should probably focus on the productivity metric. Here, a good target is to bill out at least 70% of your available hours. Even though your engineers are "always busy," the real question is whether most of their work is actually revenue-generating. (For instance, your sales folk may be giving away a lot of engineering hours to get higher prices on licensing deals.)

Also, keep an eye on how your overall corporate costs are being distributed to different departments. Your consulting group may be absorbing a lot of costs that properly belong to development or support. Ultimately, these costs are all paid out of the same company checkbook—but if you load too much onto the service group's budget, you'll never know what your real service margins are.

How should I benchmark DSO on maintenance?

"About a third of our revenue comes from maintenance contracts, and we generally send out bills at the beginning of the year for the full amount. However, many of our customers pay in quarterly installments – still in advance of the services we deliver, but theoretically many months later than the terms on our original bills. I'd like to compare our Days Sales Outstanding ratio against public company benchmarks, but I'm not sure our numbers are really comparable. Advice?"

Mike: It's always tough to benchmark against public company ratios, because these companies rarely disclose the numbers you need to drill below the surface – in your case, to see separate DSO ratios for product sales and maintenance receivables. In general, however, public companies treat receivables for future maintenance as a form of deferred revenue, and they don't include this revenue in either their top-line revenues or their DSO calculations.

For benchmarking purposes, therefore, you should also exclude maintenance receivables and the related deferred revenues when you benchmark your DSO ratio. Do this calculation quarterly and compare your numbers against quarterly public company numbers, which will smooth out some of the distortions that occur in DSO ratios that only use end-of-year numbers.

How should we allocate indirect overhead costs?

"My company has 75 employees, and recently my CFO decided we should allocate some of our G&A costs – rent, IT and help desk staff, and HR – to the individual departments and product groups that 'consume' these services. His allocation approach was simply to divide costs by the headcount in each group, which seemed reasonable. But now everyone is screaming that the formula is unfair. Any suggestions?"

Mike: It makes sense to charge back *direct* costs that managers are supposed to control. For instance, if programmers in one product group aren't fixing bugs that cause above-average tech support costs, charging the product manager's P&L for support could be a useful incentive.

But that isn't what your CFO is doing. He's allocating *indirect* costs that managers generally don't control. Worse, he's using a headcount formula that encourages the counter-productive behavior. With his approach, a manager will "save money" if he replaces regular employees with more expensive temps who aren't part of his allocation base. And that same manager will pay the same per-person occupancy costs regardless of whether he leases a spacious penthouse suite or crams his staff into 6'x6' cubicles. Even if only a few managers take advantage of these loopholes, your CFO's allocation approach is bound to cause morale problems. Tell him to try again.

Should I disclose my financials to D&B?

"I just got a call from Dun & Bradstreet, asking for a copy of my financial statements. Supposedly, publishing my numbers will help me get credit and will impress customers. Is this for real?"

Mike: I don't think many people check D&B data before doing business with an unknown company. Occasionally, a new vendor or customer may ask to see your financials, but that's best handled one-on-one in a private discussion.

Of course, some entrepreneurs like to show off how well they're doing. I know one company founder who posted the company's financial statement details (income statement, balance sheet, cash flow statement, and all revenue and expense details, including payrolls by employee) on the wall in the lobby for everyone to see — employees, customers, prospects, vendors, investors, the press, and even casual visitors. He thought full disclosure sent a message about how well he ran his company, and I have to agree.

How can we quantify future stock option expenses?

"I work for a company that's been very generous about distributing stock options to employees, so I've been watching the debate over whether or not to treat options as an expense. What I don't

understand, however, is how we're supposed to report options 'expenses' on our current financials when we never know who's going to exercise options until it happens. Can you clarify?"

Mike: Your financials probably already include several "non-cash" expense items — in particular, depreciation and bad debt reserves — that represent similar estimates of hard-to-predict costs. In essence, you'll now create a similar forecast for non-cash compensation expenses (with an offsetting adjustment in equity accounts on your balance sheet), which should reflect either your historical experience or your best guess about future events.

Since options expenses are a non-cash cost, incidentally, savvy investors aren't likely to pay much attention to whatever numbers you report here. Instead, they'll look more closely at your cash flow statements, which have become increasingly important as a reliable indicator of what's really going on with a company's finances.

Revenue Recognition & Money Mysteries

"And this is our department of experimental accounting."

When should we recognize cash revenue?

"Our single biggest client always pays us with a check dated the last day of the month, drawn on a West Coast bank. I'd like to recognize the revenue as of the date of the check (we're on a cash basis), but my bookkeeper says we have to wait until the check clears, usually five or six days later. Who's right?"

Mike: The basic accounting rule for cash-basis reporting is that you recognize revenue when you have "constructive" receipt of payment, which usually means a check in hand. The one interesting twist on this rule is that the IRS wants you to record income in the same year that your client reports the payment as a deduction. So the check he writes you on Dec. 31 should show up in your 2006 taxable income, even if you receive it several days into 2007.

But there's a much easier way to solve problems like this: Switch to accrual-basis financial reporting. With accrual accounting, you recognize revenue when you earn it and you recognize expenses when you incur them, not when you pay that bill. Of course, you'll end up with a much clearer picture of how your business is doing—and you'll eliminate the puzzling questions of cash-based accounting.

What are my intangible assets worth?

"I have a major investor who's been complaining that our balance sheet is weak. I've tried to point out that we've created major assets – in particular, technology and important reference accounts – that don't show up as the kind of assets he's used to seeing. He's not impressed. Any suggestions?"

Mike: This is a classic problem of valuation, and you'll probably have a tough time convincing your skeptical investor. In many industries, the value of a business is measured almost entirely in terms of "hard" assets—real estate, inventories, cash, receivables, and the like. Banks still take this approach, incidentally: They usually prefer to make loans based on assets that can be easily turned into cash, even though a company's real money-making assets may be intangibles like employee skills and the company's reputation. Don't even try to assign a value to intangible assets—investors and lenders won't buy your argument.

You may want to point out to your investor that acquirers rarely pay much attention to hard assets when they buy a high-tech company. The assets they care most about are customers and intellectual property. In fact, plenty of companies with weak balance sheets end up selling for amounts that can range from one to ten times revenues. Especially for an outside investor, that's the true measure of the assets you've created.

What's the value of dusty inventory?

"We have a big cage in our warehouse that's filled with obsolete versions of our software, all covered with dust. We keep this stuff on hand because occasionally a customer buys an old copy (at full list price!) for reasons of hardware compatibility, so it's 'good' inventory. But I don't feel comfortable reporting the value of these

old boxes — currently, over $100,000 — on my balance sheet. I'd like to write it all off, but then what happens when we sell a few copies?"

Mike: A good rule of thumb is that you should only carry assets on a balance sheet that have some "measurable" future value. Since you can't really predict if you'll ever sell any of this old inventory, you can legitimately write it off. (The same rule applies to very old receivables, incidentally.) When you do happen to sell a few copies, there won't be any cost of goods, so the revenue will go right to your bottom line.

Is a gift of equity a taxable transaction?

"I was planning to give three of my senior managers stock in my company, but one of them says he'd have to pay income taxes on the market value of the stock if he accepts. That seems crazy. Advice?"

Mike: He's right. If you give your managers stock, they'll wind up paying taxes on the fair market value of the stock as of the day they receive it — which could create a staggering tax bill for them.

There are several ways to avoid the tax problem if you intend the stock to be a kind of bonus. You can give them "qualified options" to buy the stock some time in the future at its current price, so they'll only be taxed on the gain (and only if they sell the shares once they exercise the options). Or you can give them "phantom stock," which entitles them to a percentage of the eventual sale price of the business. But if your plan is to give your managers real long-term equity in the business — well, the IRS considers that equity a form of income and will eventually expect to collect taxes on whatever the equity is worth.

How do I book receivables billed in advance?

"I notice that my Internet service provider and the phone company seem to be sending out bills at least 30 days before a service period begins. I'd like to do something similar for my retainer clients, but how would I record receivables on my books that aren't really due yet? And would I have to pay taxes on these receivables?"

Mike: If you can convince your clients to pay you in advance, accounting for the transaction is no problem. You simply record the amounts billed in advance on your balance sheet as "deferred revenue" (a liability), and then recognize the revenue on your income statement when you provide the service. In the software industry, for example, companies typically invoice in advance for a whole year of maintenance and then recognize the earned portion every month or quarter.

Taxes are also no problem, as long as you're reporting income on an accrual basis. Even though you've sent an invoice and perhaps even collected the cash, the revenue isn't taxable until you've earned it by delivering services or goods. (You can see why investors love companies that manage to get their customers to fund the business — there are a lot of advantages to getting paid in advance.)

Is a 'forgiven debt' taxable?

"Last year, I hired a free-lancer to rewrite our documentation. I paid him $8,000 as a down payment, but had to fire him almost immediately. Now the writer just sent me a letter saying he plans to report the $16,000 balance to the IRS as a 'forgiven debt' and he claims that amount will be taxable income to me. Can he do this?"

Mike: It's a cute idea for getting your attention, but your free-lancer is confused about how the IRS works. He can't write off (or "forgive") part of a contract payment unless he's already booked the whole value of the contract as income — which I'll bet he hasn't done. And the fact that you *didn't* spend money certainly doesn't mean you've generated taxable income for your company.

Incidentally, you might want to review why this arrangement fell apart so quickly. It's not unreasonable to pay a consultant or service provider some cash up front, but only if you have a contract or a good reason to trust the vendor's ability to perform. It sounds like you just handed over $8,000 to a near-total stranger who burned you. That's not good.

Gazing into the Crystal Ball: Budgets & Forecasts

"These projected figures are a figment of our imagination. We hope you like them."

Do business plan forecasts mean anything?

"I invested $100,000 in a new software company last year, partly because the business plan was based on the kind of detailed budget projections I've seen in big companies that I've worked for. However, I've just seen the first six months of financials, and the numbers aren't even close. Other investors seem to think this is okay, but then why did we bother with all those spreadsheets in the first place? I'm really troubled by this situation."

Mike: It's normal to see this kind of volatility during the first few years of a startup, especially compared with projections for more stable, established businesses. The reason savvy investors insist on detailed business plans is to see how well the founders understand the basic numbers that drive the business—for instance, how to put a price on the product itself and on features that customers want, how long it will take to get to market, the cost and yield of various distribution strategies, etc.

Six months is probably too early to tell if your company's founders have really screwed up in these areas. But if the company keeps missing its numbers, your fellow investors will almost certainly make any follow-on financing very expensive.

How do we make our forecasts less random?

"We have huge quarter-to-quarter revenue swings that drive me crazy. My sales reps insist all the deals in their pipeline are genuine, but our sales cycle is long — an average of six months — and they say there's no way to predict exactly when a customer will decide to sign on the dotted line. Is the situation hopeless?"

Mike: I'm a little skeptical about what you're hearing from your sales folk, but let's assume your deal pipeline really is unpredictable. One issue you need to address is how you set realistic expectations for your investors and bankers, who've probably already decided that they can't trust your revenue forecasts. I'd start by downplaying the company's quarterly bookings, which are probably governed by fairly inflexible revenue recognition rules. Instead, report on actual billings, which drive cash collections. It doesn't matter to most insiders when a customer signs a contract — the important question is how fast you collect the money from the sale. That's something you can forecast and manage with some certainty.

Of course, you'll still have uneven cash flow, so a second issue is how to make sure you can pay your bills during lean periods. I suggest you look for ways to keep monthly spending to a minimum and also put in place sufficient cash reserves (plus bank lines of credit, bridge financing, and equity financing if necessary) to cover your dry spells. Being wrong about a sales forecast is never fun, but it's unforgivable to suddenly discover you can't meet next week's payroll.

How do I develop a financial forecast for investors?

"A potential investor asked me to show him a three-year financial projection for my company. I created a spreadsheet with every cost

item and source of income I could imagine, and documented all the assumptions in the footnotes. Now the investor says this doesn't tell him enough – he wants to see 'how we get to profitability.' Is he just playing games with me?"

Mike: No, he's not playing games. The kind of spreadsheet you've created has so much detail that it obscures the relatively few big variables in running a business. Investors want to see at a glance what happens if revenues are higher or lower than you project, how your ratios compare to others in the same industry, and how long your cash will last. These are numbers you should be watching closely yourself, by the way.

I'd also dump the big spreadsheet as a way of presenting these numbers. You should always summarize your projections in standard financial format (income statement, balance sheet, cash flow) so everyone can see immediately how your month-to-month actual results compare to the original forecast. It's also a good idea to create a summary PowerPoint presentation with graphs and charts that focus on the most important changes that have occurred as the business evolves. (You can find a good set of templates for financial reporting on my Web site and in David Gumpert's book, *Burn Your Business Plan!*)

When should I update our plan?

"This may sound like a dumb question, but how often should a company update its annual business plan? A lot of things we do – including sales quotas and department budgets – are based on a forecast that's already in trouble. But if I keep changing the forecast, I know everyone will complain that we're just making up the numbers as we go along."

Mike: If you just tweak your forecast every time you hear good or bad news, the plan will seem arbitrary – and worse, the underlying financial assumptions will begin to come unstuck. The trick is to create a rock-solid schedule for getting everybody's input into a revised plan. No excuses, no missed deadlines. How often you schedule these updates depends on how fast your business is changing: Most companies revise their numbers at least quarterly, but I know of one public company that runs a new financial model each and every day.

It's also a good idea to make sure the plan always produces an answer to the question, "How much cash will we have on (you pick the date)?" If you build the plan around this question, you'll instantly see the effect of any change—for instance, a delayed product launch—and you'll know how much cash you'll need to find in cost reductions or new financing.

What's the right model for calculating lifetime value?

"Is there a standard way to calculate the 'lifetime value' of a customer? I run a custom development shop where most of our deals are in the $50,000-$200,000 range, usually from repeat customers. I'm mostly concerned with how much we should be investing to acquire and retain new clients."

Mike: Like ROI, "lifetime value" is often oversimplified — though it's an important metric to track. Here's what I suggest if you want to build a good economic model:

First, collect real data about how much average revenue you get from a new customer and how much you typically generate from follow-on business, taking into account your historical attrition rate.

Then—and this is the part that some forecasters ignore—estimate the average profit margin you're likely to generate on a year-to-year basis from this revenue stream. (If you only net $5,000 in margin on a $50,000 contract, spending $10,000 to acquire a new customer is probably not a wise move.)

Finally, apply (1) the amount you traditionally spend on marketing as a percent of your profit margin to (2) the net present value of the profit margins—this will tell you what you should plan to spend this year to generate your future revenue and profit streams.

Don't be too concerned about the accuracy of these numbers—like any sales forecast, they'll reflect a good deal of guesswork at first. But over time your estimates will get better, and eventually you'll end up with a valuable tool for making sales and marketing decisions.

How can I shorten our budget cycle?

"Aargh. We've just spent five months putting together our annual budget. Worse, this is actually faster *than usual. How can we speed up the process?"*

Mike: I don't know if it's any consolation, but budgets probably cause more agony than any other financial chore I can think of. Budgets are necessary — but there's no reason they need to be so painful. Three suggestions:

First, start with a well-designed template. A template helps you figure out the right categories, the right amount of detail, and the right relationship among the numbers. (I offer a free template on my Web site, by the way.) Using a standard template also makes it easier for the CFO's office to roll up individual department-level budgets into one company-wide budget.

Second, get started earlier — much earlier. Any budget that's finalized five months into the year will be very, very stale. To speed up the budget process, deliver the templates two months before the fiscal year begins. At that time, you should also get general buy-in on a revenue forecast for next year and how much spending on headcount and new operations the company can justify. Based on those numbers, ask your department managers to deliver a first pass on their individual budgets within three weeks. Obviously, these preliminary budgets won't have much detail. But you'll be able to quickly spot managers who seem determined to overspend.

Third, don't use the budget to micro-manage. I see budgets all the time that show line items for every magazine subscription and pizza party. This is just silly. Your managers should focus on how much money they need within broad categories, and should have discretionary power to move money around within these categories during the year. Overall, the important goal for any budget is to make sure your spending and productivity ratios are in line with company strategy and industry benchmarks. If your managers consistently meet these targets, that's all you really need to know.

How can I teach employees the value of money?

"Many people in my company seem to feel that if there's 'money in the budget' for an expenditure, they have a duty to spend it all — even if they can get a better deal with a little haggling. I keep telling our employees that their budgets won't be cut next year, but nobody — absolutely nobody — seems to believe me. How can I persuade people to be more frugal?"

Mike: The first thing to remember is that you are dealing with a cultural issue, not a financial issue. Take a look around: Do people get raises and promotions because they manage big budgets? Did the company pay for pin striping the CEO's car? Do sales people and developers collect bonuses even when they consistently miss targets? Believe me, this kind of behavior sends a message that being frugal isn't part of the company's mission statement.

You probably need to take drastic steps to make your company's culture more cost-sensitive. Start with a bottoms-up budget process for next year. Make your department heads justify every major expense — not just the increase they want, but the expense itself. Compare spending by category, region and manager to last year's actual spending, and have everyone work as a group to drive down costs. For example, ask your managers to rank all their employees and to be prepared to cull out non-performers. (You don't need to implement actual layoffs — you just want managers to identify the deadwood.)

Finally, put in place a company-wide bonus scheme that rewards everyone for beating *both* the revenue and the earnings targets. You won't change corporate culture overnight, but setting clear, measurable goals will point people in the right direction.

How do we move from cost-per-unit budgets to revenue percentages?

"We have a new CEO, who is a firm believer in keeping our costs in line with industry benchmarks. He keeps saying, 'Explain why everyone else can do the job for X% of sales when you say you need 2X%.' He has a valid point, but our budgets have always been based on our own historical models – mostly, cost per units sold. We're completely lost about how to make the transition. Any advice?"

Mike: Making this kind of shift in accounting approaches is always hard. At the very least, you should go back a year and convert your cost numbers from your old per-unit calculations to the percentage-of-sales approach your CEO wants. Don't worry about converting your small expenses – concentrate on the big items that probably make up 80% of your cost structure.

Incidentally, your CEO is absolutely right to insist on this exercise. Using cost-per-unit numbers for budgeting is great when your operations are stable. It's easy for everyone to understand, and it helps you focus your thinking on how cost reduction tactics affect your potential profit on the products you sell. Unfortunately, per-unit costing is less helpful whenever your sales rise or fall quickly. Fixed costs – rent, many of your salaries, and other overhead – don't vary according to the number of units you sell. So your benchmarking comparisons go out of whack.

Moreover, most companies use some variation of the percentage of sales approach for major cost items like sales and marketing, R&D, and overhead, so you can easily compare your spending to industry benchmarks and your own prior results.

How do we know if a project-based business is profitable?

"We usually have four or five big projects going on at once, so our month-to-month revenues and profits are very uneven. For the first

six months of this year, we thought all of our projects were in the black — but it turns out that we actually lost a fair amount of money, mostly because of overhead costs that weren't reflected in our project accounting. Can you suggest a way to tie project margins more closely to our company income statement?"

Mike: This is essentially a forecasting problem. You should be reviewing each project at least once a month (preferably more often) to project how much profit it's likely to contribute to your corporate bottom line. If there's a profit problem, you'll be able to catch it early enough to work out a fix.

As part of your forecast, you also need to know exactly what your fixed overhead costs actually are — your monthly "nut." These costs include items like rent, staff salaries, utilities, insurance, and anything else that you'd have to pay even if you didn't have any active projects. Many people who run project-based businesses underestimate these costs, and so they're caught by surprise when the money they make on individual projects doesn't cover their total overhead costs.

Should we kill an out-of-control project?

"We have a new product under development that's already 50% over budget, with no end in sight. I'd like to kill the project, but my R&D manager thinks we should keep going 'so we'll have a chance to recover our investment.' This debate is tearing the company apart. Can you suggest an objective, non-emotional way to decide who's right?"

Mike: No matter what you do, you and your R&D manager are arguing about the future — which means you're both making assumptions that may or may not be true. However, you can test your assumptions objectively by creating two fairly simple spreadsheets. The first is a cash flow analysis for the company, with and without the project. In one scenario, you stop the project today and write off the investment. In the second scenario, you continue the project through the point that it begins to generate positive cash flow. This analysis — which should include a large buffer for future cost overruns as well as a marketing budget for the launch — will help you determine if you can even afford to finish the product. If the project puts the whole company at risk, that should be the end of the discussion.

The second spreadsheet will measure the product's value proposition, assuming you decide to proceed. Paying back development costs is not enough: A reasonable standard for software is that a new product should be able to return at least 25 times its development costs within three years. If your R&D manager can't make a plausible case for that kind of payback, you're probably better off investing your development dollars in other projects.

Is it safe to sell fixed-price services contracts?

"According to my marketing people, our customers want us to promise a fixed price on custom installation work. But the one time we tried this approach, the customer made so many changes that we lost our shirts on the project. Do you know a way that we can protect ourselves?"

Mike: The best way to protect yourself (and to set reasonable customer expectations) is to write a very clear, detailed "scope of services" description. Don't get lazy here — you need to spell out exactly what you're proposing to do for the customer, and what the specific acceptance criteria are. If there's any gray area — for example, if no one is sure how many hours of training will be needed to get users up to speed — you should break out that item as a separate time and materials cost, to be billed separately.

Make sure your project managers are consistently careful about change orders, too. It's easy to slip into bad habits and agree to undocumented freebies. Once the job is done, you'll *never* collect a dime on cost overruns unless you can prove the customer signed off on the extras.

You also need to make sure your fixed price is actually profitable. You need to track every job to see if your forecasts of gross margin were on target, and ideally you should base your sales commissions on profitability, not on gross dollars.

Managing Expenses

"Well, gentlemen, there's your problem."

Should I pay for parking tickets?

"This isn't a big deal, but I have a couple of engineers who always get parking tickets when they visit a downtown client. They put the tickets on their expense accounts, and they've suggested that I bill the client for these 'expenses.' Would this be proper?"

Mike: The dollars may not be big, but the principle — the fact that the company is reimbursing employees for illegal acts — is quite serious. If you make excuses for small transgressions, eventually some of your employees may decide to raise the ante with under-the-table payoffs, small bribes, and hidden slush funds. Certainly, not every company that winks at parking tickets becomes another Enron. But setting strict rules about small things is a good way to ensure that employees make the right decisions on the big issues.

As for billing the customer — presumably, you're thinking about hiding parking tickets in a category like "travel expenses." If the customer ever asks for an itemization, would you be comfortable explaining what you've tried to get away with? If not, tell your engineers to find a parking garage.

Should we pay consultants for their travel time?

"My company has a big project that requires outside consultants to come in for a few days at a time every month. Two of our consultants fly in from Chicago, and I see on their first bill that they're charging us for four hours of travel time each way, at their full billing rate. We never discussed this issue when we hired them, so I feel very awkward about challenging the bill. But it's going to add up to a lot of money for the total project. Is paying for travel time a standard practice?"

Mike: There really isn't a standard practice for travel payments, but many consultants feel that they have a limited inventory of billable hours and don't feel they should give away time they could otherwise sell. This is especially true when a consultant has to spend long stretches of time in transit—say, eight hours of travel for a two-hour meeting.

But why is this issue surfacing now? Most professional consultants will address issues like this in an engagement letter, which both sides should look over before the assignment begins. It's pretty unprofessional to skip this step, and you might be able to negotiate a reduction in travel billing if your consultants failed to mention their policy in advance.

Is there a way to deal with late expense reports?

"What should I do when sales people in my company submit expense reports that are six to nine months late? This is a delicate question, because our CEO does the same thing – in fact, I just wrote him a check for more than $20,000, right after I closed the books on our fiscal year."

Mike: There's a simple solution: Just record a very large reserve on your balance sheet for outstanding expense reports. This will be a polite reminder to your CEO (and perhaps to your board) that expenses should be submitted in a timely fashion. Even if you don't get his support, at least you're being loaned a fair amount of money at 0% interest.

Of course, you'll still have a problem with any expenses that are charged back to customers, who probably don't like getting invoices for expenses incurred nine months ago. Here, you might try a policy that says billable expenses won't be reimbursed if they're submitted late. If your customers are complaining, that will certainly help you make your case.

Should I pay commissions to our purchasing agents?

"As part of a reorganization, our purchasing department now reports to me. I've discovered that the purchasing agents get a bonus based on how much they negotiate down a vendor's bid (25% of the discount). Is this a normal arrangement?"

Mike: I've heard of this approach, but it's definitely not a standard arrangement. In fact, I think it's truly a dumb idea. Once your vendors figure out what you're doing—and they always figure it out—they'll simply inflate their bids and then "negotiate" down. You've eliminated any incentive for vendors to start with a fair price, or even their lowest price.

And what happens when the time comes to renew a contract? Over time, vendors usually get more cost-efficient and can gradually reduce their prices. But saving a few points on a renewal contract usually won't produce significant commissions for your purchasing agents, so they'll probably leave that money on the table. My advice: Dump this incentive plan as fast as you can.

How can we keep our office rent under control?

"We've had a 15-year lease on our office space that, because of cost of living escalators, eventually put our rent way above current market prices. I won't do that again, but I'm also nervous about having to renegotiate or move every few years if we sign short leases. Any advice on how we can protect ourselves in this situation?"

Mike: Technology companies always seem to be either outgrowing their offices or trying to get rid of extra space. Unless you're unusually confident about your future business and staffing needs, your best strategy is to stay clear of long-term commitments and instead focus on negotiating flexible renewal terms. Landlords are pretty hungry right now, so you're probably in a good bargaining position.

Another approach would be for you to buy a building and sublease any space you don't immediately need. However, that strategy puts you in the real estate business — which is almost certainly not your core expertise.

How do I explain the concept of profits?

"Our revenues are up dramatically this year, and everyone is talking about bonuses and new funding for pet projects. Trouble is, our margins are still tight and we have very little cash. I honestly don't think my employees understand the difference between revenues and profits. How can I teach them about basic business economics?"

Mike: I find it's helpful to relate company finances to your employees' personal financial activities. You can point out that someone who "earns" $1,000 a week probably spends most of that money on taxes, health insurance, mortgage payments, food, kids, etc. Usually, they have very little "profit" left over for fun stuff like vacations and hobbies. Ask people how much spare cash they had left over the last time they were given a raise — that usually drives the point home.

You might also want to open the company's books, at least part way, to show why money isn't as available as your employees think. You could have your CFO lead a lunch-time training session on the company's financial current and forecast financial situation, including the balance sheet, income statement, profits and cash flows. This is a popular approach among early-stage companies whose financial situation is volatile. And if you really want to teach business finance, I know of at least one company that invites rank-and-file employees to prepare presentations for the rest of the staff on each quarter's key numbers. When you're forced to field questions about your own presentation, you really have to know your stuff.

What costs can I cut without controversy?

"I've been trying to cut costs around the office, but it seems like everything I propose — most recently, eliminating free coffee and soda — creates a huge controversy. Are there costs I can cut that no one will notice?"

Mike: Probably, but that won't solve the problem. The best way I know to save money is for the top person in the company — typically, the CEO — to show that cost-cutting is a top priority, and to get very visibly involved in every discussion that involves money, from raises to expense accounts. (Of course, the CEO can't fly first class when everyone else flies coach.) Once it's clear that the boss is genuinely concerned about saving money, most employees will jump on the bandwagon.

In addition, you should take a hard look at your three or four biggest expense areas, not just the nickle-and-dime stuff. For a technology company, salaries, rent, and travel usually represent about 75% of the company's spending. Look for creative alternatives — part-time staffing, moving to cheaper space, less travel, competitive bids from major suppliers. If you can squeeze even 10% out of your largest expense categories, you'll find the cost savings will be quite dramatic.

How do I find out what insurance I really need?

"Is there someone who can independently audit our insurance coverage? My insurance agent obviously wants us to buy every policy in the book, but I know some of what he's pitching is unnecessary. I just can't spend the time it will take to do a proper job of researching all our options."

Mike: I have a Rolodex full of experts, but nobody who audits insurance policies. That's too bad, because — as you've discovered — this is a very complicated subject. Most senior people in companies seem to rely on their friendly agents to renew coverage that's been in place for years. I think that's unwise, especially if there's a chance you won't be covered properly if there's a serious claim against you.

If you're concerned about your present coverage, somehow you'll have to find time to educate yourself about what kind of coverage is "usual and customary" for your industry, who are the major providers, and what it costs. Talk to CFOs at other companies and ask two or three independent agents to put together some recommendations, and follow up by getting competitive quotes. It's a tough job, but you'll sleep better at night.

What happens when a vendor's sales rep lies?

"I'm in a seemingly-endless battle with a big telecom company. Their sales rep – who has since vanished – promised free installation and other services that the company never provided. The money isn't really worth going to court over (I think they're counting on this, in fact), but I'm curious about the bigger question of whether a company can simply walk away from commitments made by its sales reps. Your thoughts?"

Mike: Sadly, you always see a big jump in dubious behavior whenever the economy gets tight. Salespeople start to make more "unauthorized commitments" (a polite term) to close deals they desperately need, and fewer companies will go ahead and honor those commitments for the sake of customer good will. This is definitely a time to get *every* promise in writing, and especially to read the fine print in the contract about what happens if you have to pull the plug on a dishonest vendor.

Graceful Exits

"So, Jim, where do you see yourself in ten minutes?"

How can I optimize my company's value?

"I'd like to sell my company some day for the best possible price (we develop vertical market software), but I'm baffled by the big variations in valuation I see. Some companies seem to be worth a lot because of their technology, others because of customers, others because of market share — it's all over the map. If I had one good metric to aim for, I could probably optimize my company's long-term value significantly. Suggestions?"

Mike: This may be just a hard-nosed accountant's point of view, but I'm convinced that your best single goal should be high, profitable sales. If you have high sales, it's pretty clear that you have good technology ("good" being defined as what customers will pay for). High sales also means your market share is growing and so is your customer base — qualities that buyers like to see.

Remember, though, that you must achieve high sales within

the limits of your resources (i.e., you must be profitable), and you can't run out of cash. If you look at sellers who get *low* valuations, it's almost always because they were having trouble paying bills and meeting payroll.

What's a zero-revenue company worth?

"Our investors just pulled the plug on our financing, leaving us with a more-or-less finished product we can't afford to launch. We don't have any debt on the books, but we also don't have any revenues. I think I know people who'd pay a fair price to acquire the work we've done, and I'm willing to invest a few more months trying to put together a deal. However, I don't want to waste my time if buyers are just going to offer me a dollar 'to take the business off my hands.' Your advice?"

Mike: Start talking immediately to all the likely suspects, and be very clear about your timetable. (People who sell businesses are sometimes amazingly secretive about their goals and timing.) You'll find out pretty quickly if there's any interest, and what kind of valuation is realistic. Considering how many Internet companies have found buyers lately, I think you might find a reasonable deal.

At the same time, even an eager buyer needs time for due diligence. So you should work to extend your runway by making your cash last longer. In this case, your goal is to preserve whatever assets will be most valuable to the ultimate buyer—probably your core development team. Don't waste precious cash paying marketing and admin people who'll probably get axed anyway when a buyer takes over.

How do I avoid pre-sale gossip?

"I'd like to sell my company, but I'm worried that the people I plan to approach—including two major competitors—will spread rumors about my plans. That's bound to affect the morale of my employees and will probably wreck my sales. Your advice?"

Mike: Before you open your books or get into any substantive talks, you definitely need to get potential buyers — especially competitors — to sign a non-disclosure agreement. Gossip about the sale can cause serious long-term damage, which almost certainly will be reflected in a downward price adjustment at the closing and a lower earnout payment (if that's how the deal is structured).

Of course, a certain amount of gossip can also make you look like a hot acquisition candidate and may even attract buyers you didn't think were interested. Once you sign a term sheet with a no-shop clause you can't discuss the deal with anyone else, but up to that point a little publicity may actually help your bargaining position.

Do you recommend a sale of assets?

"A potential buyer for my company has said he'd like to buy all our assets — products, receivables, customer lists, etc. — and leave us with the corporate shell. This seems okay: We'd pay off our loans and distribute the cash from the sale to our own shareholders, just as if we'd sold our stock. Am I missing something?"

Mike: No, you're not missing anything. In fact, asset sales are quite common these days, because they're a simple way for buyers to protect themselves from undisclosed liabilities and other nasty surprises. If you were to sell the whole corporation, moreover, the buyer would probably hold back a portion of the purchase price for a few years to cover these liabilities. And chances are, you'd be asked to indemnify the buyer if the holdback wasn't enough. With an asset sale, you're more likely to get all your selling price up front.

How do we value a customer list?

"We've been in discussions with a company that wants to acquire us, and they've said our most important asset is probably our customer list. Trouble is, we can't agree on a valuation formula for the list — and I don't want to show them the list until we agree on the pricing. Any suggestions?"

Mike: If you have a relatively small number of active customers — usually, less than a hundred — there's no real "formula" for valuing your customer list. Chances are, any would-be buyer will have a pretty good idea of who your customers are and how much revenue they represent. If you're really pressed, you might want to prepare a list of your top dozen or so clients (without names) and an indication of how much revenue they each generated in the past year.

If you have a very large number of *small* customers — for instance, companies that buy a subscription service like payroll processing — then you can adapt the RFM ("recency, frequency, money") formula that mailing list brokers use to value customer lists. If you can show that you have a high proportion of long-term customers with an active purchasing history, your list is clearly a valuable asset.

Will my salary dilute an acquirer's EPS?

"I've been talking with a potential buyer for my company (which I own completely), who says the price they'll pay is low because we're barely profitable. I pointed out that I've chosen to take out my profits as salary — $310,000 last year — to avoid double taxation. His answer, basically, is that our low profits will 'dilute' his company's reported earnings, so he can't budge on price. Is this just a negotiating tactic?"

Mike: Yes, this is a negotiating tactic. Believe me, before making any kind of offer, your buyer ran the pro forma numbers to see what the deal looked like without your salary and other post-transaction costs he plans to eliminate. And when he shows the deal to his own shareholders, public or private, he'll use these pro forma numbers to show the future impact on earnings per share — because the future is what matters in an acquisition, not the past.

Is it ethical to leave a company that's being sold?

"I'm about to close a deal to sell my company to a larger competitor. The buyer wants to lock me and my top managers into a very tough non-compete, which ordinarily we wouldn't mind. However, after our investors get paid off, I can see that there will be nothing but chump change left for the founders. Rather than go through all the

stress of a buyout and get tied down by a non-compete, I'm beginning to think that we'd be better off just quitting and letting the investors salvage what they can. Would that be ethical?"

Mike: This is a tough call. As an employee and as a founder, you do have an implied obligation to do whatever it takes to protect shareholder value. Especially if your departure wrecks the deal, moreover, you could have real problems in the future convincing other investors (or employers) that you can be trusted.

But I also think there's something odd going on here. In every company sale I've seen, the investors were always careful to keep the management team happy (usually through new option arrangements with the acquirer). I suggest you have a heart-to-heart talk with your investors about your future with the new company. Chances are, you and your management team are on the expendable list — and if that's the case, you should jump ship sooner rather than later.

Can I prevent a buyer from stealing my employees?

"I gave a potential buyer for my company the resumes for all of my employees — 20 people altogether. I just found out he's had several conversations with my vice president of sales. The buyer says this is a standard due diligence practice, but I'm worried that he'll decide it's cheaper to steal my best people. How do I protect myself?"

Mike: Usually, buyers sign a term sheet or letter of intent that includes a clause prohibiting them from soliciting your employees during due diligence. Since you don't have a written agreement yet, you should immediately talk with the buyer about your objections. This could be a deal-killer, but otherwise your buyer could go on to pick the brains of every manager (and perhaps every employee) in your company. At the very least, you can insist that all conversations take place with you present.

Even non-solicitation clauses may not fully protect you against an unscrupulous buyer. I know one large software company that tried to steal key employees during merger talks by pitching their *spouses* on the benefits on jumping ship—technically, not a violation of the non-solicitation agreement. If you spot even a hint of unethical behavior, it's always a good idea to look more closely at a would-be buyer's reputation.

Can a seller solicit competing M&A bids?

"We recently signed a letter of intent to acquire a small competitor. Now I hear that one of their board members is still talking 'unofficially' with a rival bidder. Is this ethical?"

Mike: It all depends on whether the letter of intent included a "no shop" provision. If it does, the seller is absolutely prohibited from soliciting other offers. It's unethical and a breach of contract, even if the solicitation is "unofficial." Ask your lawyer or M&A representative to discuss the rumor with the seller's CEO, who should promptly put an end to these discussions.

Naturally, if you didn't include a no-shop clause in your letter of intent, all bets are off. In fact, the seller's directors have an ongoing obligation to get the best price for their company, and they have a right to talk with rival bidders until the final deal is consummated.

How do I persuade a buyer to invest in growth?

"I negotiated an earnout when I sold my company, but six months after the merger the parent company started chopping our budget for R&D, lead generation, customer service, etc. Of course, profits will go up for a while—but eventually these idiotic decisions will wreck the business (and my earnout). How can I convince the new management to invest properly in the company's ongoing development?"

Mike: In an ideal world, you'd have a killer product that the buyer's sales force could sell with their eyes closed, and you'd have total control over the product line that drives the revenue used in the earnout calculations. Failing that, you'd have a buyer who's eager to do whatever is "fair" to protect you from losing money from a change in the company's investment priorities. If you don't feel you have this kind of ideal product or ideal buyer, I'd be pretty reluctant to trade any up-front money for the promise of an earnout.

However, bear in mind that sellers are sometimes partly to blame when a buyer under-funds an acquisition. If it turns out that you exaggerated your company's likely revenue or profit contribution, a rational buyer will eventually shift most of your funding to competing product lines that promise a higher ROI. And in extreme cases, the buyer may try to recover as much cash as possible from the deal by chopping costs to the bone and selling off assets at fire-sales prices. To make sure you get the backing you need for your earnout, you need to demonstrate that your operation is one of the buyer's highest-performing investments.

What if my buyer is lazy about receivables?

"I've been asked to leave part of the purchase price of my company in escrow, to guarantee that my receivables are collectible. That seems reasonable in theory, but how do I know if the buyer will aggressively pursue slow accounts if he can just tap the escrow any time there are difficulties?"

Mike: The basic test is whether both sides expect to keep doing business with each other. Start by contacting all the customers who owe significant amounts to make sure they're satisfied with your company's products and services. If not, there's a good chance they'll use the transition as an excuse to jump ship and leave behind some unpaid bills — exactly the reason that the acquirer wants you to guarantee your receivables.

You also need to explore the acquirer's own plans for your customer base. If the new owners plan to abandon products, close sales offices, or eliminate long-standing discounts — at least some of your customers will be ticked off enough to withhold payments. If the acquirer isn't committed to your customer base, then you should be very cautious about guaranteeing the company's receivables.

How do we pay off missing shareholders?

"We have more than 20 ex-employees who were given small amounts of stock during my company's early days. We're about to sell the business, so they're entitled to cash payments for their shares. The problem is, we don't have current addresses for most of these people. What do I do with the cash for the shareholders I can't find?"

Mike: If there's no surviving business, just park the money in a checking account. You need to make a good faith effort to track down your missing shareholders (the Internet is a handy tool for finding people, incidentally). Eventually, the money will revert to the state under so-called "escheat" laws and you'll have no further obligations.

Do buyers have to honor a seller's promises?

"I spent almost a year working my butt off to get my company's finances in shape to be sold. My boss, the CEO, promised I'd be 'taken care of' by the new owners. But now he's gone and the new owners have already announced that there won't be any bonuses or options grants for at least a year. Do I have any recourse?"

Mike: Not really. Almost certainly, your former CEO pocketed a higher sale price by neglecting to tell the buyers about his promises. An honest seller would have protected his employees with things like accelerated stock option vesting, retention bonuses, guaranteed employment continuation, or salary adjustments. If these rewards imposed an ongoing cost on the buyer — such as higher salaries for key employees — the buyer almost certainly would have negotiated a lower price for the company. Clearly, that didn't happen.

A Few Questions I Never Got Around to Answering

"My company recently sent $50,000 to the love child of a former Nigerian oil minister who has $200 million in a secret bank account. We're going to get 25% of this account for helping her transfer the funds to the U.S. (plus the expense money we advanced). But I have serious misgivings about this project. My CFO says we should classify the $50,000 as an R&D expense, and perhaps capitalize it. I think we're better off calling it a 'business development' item and putting it in the sales and marketing budget. Who's right?"

"I plan to burn down my building and collect the insurance money. But I don't want the amount of insurance coverage I have to look suspiciously large. Are there any standard financial ratios that would help me plan this project?"

"We always seem to come up a few hundred dollars short every month when we reconcile our bank deposits. My bookkeeper says this is a 'technical' problem that isn't 'material' to the business, so I should butt out and let him handle it. He certainly sounds convincing, but we've had the same problem for three years now. Is there any way for me to create a sense of urgency with him?"

"I've been hiding unpaid bills in my garage to make my company look more profitable. Now my wife says there's no room to park the car. Can you suggest a better hiding place?"

"My bookkeeper is a complete idiot. Is this normal?"

"My controller tells me that a Chinese Feng Shui expert says that his work area is not oriented properly for 'prosperity,' but we can solve the problem by giving him a corner office with a better view. Should he face East or West?"

"Didn't you used to work at Arthur Andersen?"

Index of Questions

Do you recommend a sale of assets?
How do we value a customer list?
Will my salary dilute an acquirer's EPS?
Is it ethical to leave a company that' being sold?
Can I prevent a buyer from stealing my employees?
Can a seller solicit competing M&A bids?
How do I persuade a buyer to invest in growth?
What if my buyer is lazy about receivables?
How do we pay off missing shareholders?
Do buyers have to honor a seller's promises?

Finance expert Michael Gonnerman has been a trusted advisor to hundreds of technology CEOs and investors and has served on more than two dozen corporate boards. A frequent speaker on entrepreneurship, Mike is well known for his pragmatic, candid solutions to problems of operations and cash management.

Danyelle Desjardins

www.gonnerman.com

Visit Mike's Web site for the following resources:

Sign up for a free subscription to the *Ask Mike* e-mail newsletter and see the latest answers to tough questions about entrepreneurial finance and management.

Test your Financial IQ with these twenty questions that every CEO and investor should be able to answer.

Download Mike's free management tools and templates—

- agenda for a Board of Directors meeting
- corporate investment policy
- monthly financial report, including numbers, graphs and text
- cap table generator
- integrated financial model
- five-year financial projection template
- dashboard report
- financial bonus calculator

Read 99 *Ways to Increase Cash* and other useful articles.

Michael Gonnerman Inc.
65 Washington Drive
Sudbury, Mass. 01776
978/443-1340
www.gonnerman.com